WINETRIPPING

YOUR GUIDE TO THE BEST WINERIES
OF BRITISH COLUMBIA:
OKANAGAN & SIMILKAMEEN

RACHEL VON STURMER

D0926243

Copyright © 2016 by Rachel von Sturmer. All rights reserved.
Cover Design: Laurie Millotte
Cover Illustration: Rafael Varona
Photography: Rachel von Sturmer
First edition published: 2016

LIBRARY AND ARCHIVES CANADA CATALOGUING IN PUBLICATION
von Sturmer, Rachel, author
Winetripping: Your Guide to the Best Wineries of British Columbia -
Okanagan & Similkameen
ISBN: 978-0-9952352-0-5
1. Wineries - British Columbia - Okanagan Valley, Similkameen Valley
(Region) - Guidebooks 2. Wine tourism - British Columbia - Okanagan
Valley, Similkameen Valley (Region) 3. British Columbia - Guidebooks

No part of this publication may be reproduced, stored in a retrieval
system, or transmitted in any form of by any means, be they elec-
tronic, mechanical, photocopying, recording, or otherwise, except for
brief statements for the purpose of review, without the prior written
consent of the author. For more information, visit rachelvonsturmer.-
com. The information in this book is true and complete to the best
of the author's knowledge, and reasonable care has been taken in its
preparation. The author makes no warranty about the accuracy or
completeness of the content of this book, and disclaims all liability
from its use.

Thank you to my kind, funny, & generous husband Deacon, the best
road trip partner in the world.

To the wineries of the beautiful Okanagan & Similkameen valleys,
thank you for your passionate commitment to crafting delicious
wines.

CONTENTS

INTRODUCTION

The natural beauty of our wine country is going to leave a mark on your heart. Whether it's watching the clouds shift and shape their way across the sky, the views over one of the many lakes, or a vista of vineyards and orchards, it's glorious up here.

The Okanagan/Similkameen is on the verge of something very special, with a dynamic energy that I think you're going to really enjoy. Every winery is doing something unique and having fun doing it, whether it's perfecting Riesling, experimenting with concrete eggs, or building their winery out of straw bales (with goats on the roof to boot). The wines are delicious.

This book is the result of hundreds of winery visits, and over a thousand different wines sampled. Many of the wineries featured in this book are small to mid-sized. You're going to love the passion these producers put into their wine, and in creating a welcoming and unique atmosphere for you in their tasting rooms. I'm excited to support these businesses, many of which are family-run and making strides in sustainable farming and production. I've also included several big names, as they have the budgets to put together some amazing tours, tastings, and event experiences for you.

Since we're a young wine region and don't yet have a full set of official sub-appellations drawn up, I've listed several zones where wineries are clustered together, perfect for winetripping. Wineries are organized alphabetically within each area for handy reference. I've crafted my descriptions to give an honest sense of what to expect from each producer, and to help you choose the ones most appealing to you.

In the appendices, you'll find a build-your-own adventure section, where wineries are grouped into different categories along with several suggested itineraries for creating your own winetripping tours, plus space to jot down your favourites as you go.

Some details about the winery listings:

- PP is "per person".

- Prices listed are an approximate guide of the cost range per bottle.

- WWP means that tasting fees are "waived with wine purchase". Many wineries will WWP, and those who don't will often donate the proceeds to charitable causes.

- **Tasting room hours listed are based on high season (June-early Sept), so consult websites off season; some wineries may stop pouring 15 minutes prior to closing time. Times are subject to change.**

- **Asterisks (*) have been added beside the names of highly recommended producers.**

Happy winetripping!

Rachel

PS: please do let me know about your adventures and travels on Instagram @rachelvonsturmer & Twitter @rachelvonwine using #winetripping. I can't wait to hear about your discoveries.

OKANAGAN VALLEY

Prepare to be amazed at the sheer natural beauty and variety of wines to enjoy in this long lake filled valley, where every winery has something special to offer.

From the deserts of Osoyoos in the south, to the sweet dried herb scented Black Sage bench, vivid Golden Mile, scenic Skaha Lake, winery packed Naramata, rolling hills of Summerland and Peachland, to the monumental wineries of Kelowna, and majestic Lake Country, welcome to winetripping the Okanagan.

OSOYOOS

The hottest sub-region of the Okanagan is Osoyoos, which enjoys desert heat, and where pool weather arrives in April. Prepare to slow down to allow rattlesnakes to cross the road, and taste some of the ripest reds in the valley.

ADEGA ON 45th

7311 45 St, Osoyoos
(250)495-6243
www.adegaon45.com
Tasting room: Daily 10-5
Tasting fee: Complimentary
Wine Prices: $18-48

Tucked into the hill on the way to Nk'Mip Resort, this ochre stucco winery is a favourite of locals who are hooked on their tasty estate grown wines. It's run by a family with Portuguese heritage, a*dega* meaning winery. This is a place where everyone leaves carrying a bottle or a box.

Pop in for well made and flavourful whites (Chardonnay, Pinot Gris, Viognier), and ripe, bold reds (Syrah, Merlot, Malbec). Make sure to try their award winning Quarteto Tinto, a Bordeaux-inspired blend (Cabernet Sauvignon, Cabernet Franc, Merlot, and Malbec), and their reserve line of Syrah and Merlot. They have a popular off-dry rosé which would be perfect for sipping on the sunny patio overlooking Osoyoos Lake, the warmest fresh-water lake in Canada.

Fruit is carefully grown on their estate, and they also sell their in-demand grapes to other wineries. The tasting room has a relaxed and friendly vibe, and you're welcome to relax and enjoy a snack from their deli cooler (cheese, salami, pate, olives), or bring your own picnic.

LARIANA CELLARS

8310 2nd Ave, Osoyoos
(250)498-9259
www.larianacellars.com
Tasting room: Daily 11-4
Tasting fee: Complimentary
Wine Prices: $25-45

This niche quality-minded producer is a little out of the way, close to the US border, but making serious waves for their focused portfolio of stand-out Viognier, Carmenere, plus top tier red blend named after the vintage, such as "Thirteen" (Cab Sauv, Syrah, Carmenere).

It's a garagiste tasting room, so if you're popping in and the winery's not staffed, call and someone can come in from the vineyards to pour for you.

*LA STELLA WINERY

8123 148th Ave, Osoyoos
(250)495-8180
www.lastella.ca
Tasting room: Daily 10:30-6:30

Tasting fee: $10 pp WWP of $35 & $18 pp WWP of $80
Wine Prices: $20-130

Pulling up to this upscale winery you might be reminded of the Italian countryside. This is *the* place to come for Super Tuscan-style reds, which have amassed quite the loyal following. All housed in a pretty building that will transport you to Tuscany. You can even contemplate the dolce vita lifestyle from their balcony tables.

Start with a sip of the Moscato D'Osoyoos, floral and lightly sweet, the Leggiero, an unoaked Chardonnay, or the Vivace, made from Pinot Grigio. The reds are tannic, sometimes intense wines that have a structure that rewards aging, such as the Fortissimo (Merlot, Sangiovese, Cab Sauv, and Cab Franc), or Maestoso Merlot.

The tasting room staff are knowledgeable, friendly, and solicitous, and the bar is a perfect place to sip and watch the sun set over Osoyoos Lake. This is the sister winery to Le Vieux Pin on the Black Sage Bench, with the same talented winemaker, Severine Pinte.

*MOON CURSER VINEYARDS

3628 HWY 3 East, Osoyoos
(250)495-5161
www.mooncurser.com
Tasting room: Daily 10-5
Tasting fee: $5 pp WWP
Wine Prices: $22-43

A must visit for Osoyoos winetrippers, these passionate renegades are known for their unusual selection of grape varietals. This friendly winery overlooks Osoyoos Lake, and is sure to impress you with their quirky, tasty whites and smooth, bold, concentrated reds. The fun labels and name of the winery reflect the gold mining history in the valley, when prospectors would wait for

a moonless night to sneak their gold past customs agents at the nearby border.

For whites, try the refreshing Italian variety Arneis, or their Rhone Valley inspired Afraid of the Dark blend (Roussanne, Viognier, and Marsanne). Moon Curser are perhaps best known for their red wines, which in the strong heat are able to ripen appealingly. The Syrah is a winner, as are the Malbec, Tempranillo, Carmenere, Touriga Nacional, and inky dark Petit Verdot. They also do a signature red Bordeaux-style blend called Border Vines (Merlot, Cabernet Sauv, Malbec, Petit Verdot and Carmenere).

NK'MIP CELLARS

1400 Rancher Creek Rd, Osoyoos
(250)495-2985
www.nkmipcellars.com
Tasting room: Daily 9-8
Restaurant: The Patio - Daily 11:30-4
Tasting fee: $3-10 pp
Wine Prices: $17-68

This winery is located on the bench just east of Osoyoos Lake. Keep an eye out for rattlesnakes and sagebrush as you arrive at one of the classiest resorts in Osoyoos, created by the

Osoyoos Indian Band. The winery has a great selection of First Nations art and history.

You'll be greeted by a well appointed tasting bar which looks into the winemaking area, and has a wide selection of whites and reds. You're sure to find a favourite among the many varieties, including Chardonnay, and Pinot Blanc, or popular blend Dream-catcher. The Riesling Icewine's a stunner. The reds in particular will show you how well the desert heat can ripen grapes, which characteristic smooth tannins on the Merlot, Pinot Noir, Syrah, Cab Sauv.

If you have time for lunch, the restaurant's grassy patio has the best lake views in the area. Onsite, the resort offers full service accommodation, a pool and hot tub area, spa, Sonora Dunes golf course, and NK'MIP Desert Cultural Centre.

OLIVER

A place that calls itself "The Wine Capital of Canada" has got to be good, and in many ways Oliver is the heart of the Okanagan. There are enough big names here, plus smaller niche producers, to keep you winetripping for days.

For the purposes of this guide, I've divided the region in to two parts: The Golden Mile area for the west side of the valley, named for our first official wine sub-appellation or Sub-Geographical Indication (GI); and, the Black Sage Bench area for the east side of the valley (it'll likely be our next sub-GI).

GOLDEN MILE AREA

On the hills to the west of Okanagan Highway 97, just south of Oliver, you'll spot the wineries of the Golden Mile area, which has some of the most special terroir in the Okanagan. Those hills, which get full exposure to morning sun and allow frosty air to sink into the valley below, used to house gold mines.

In order to put Golden Mile on their label, grapes must be grown exclusively in the area.

*C.C. JENTSCH CELLARS

4522 HWY 97, Oliver
(778)439-2091
www.ccjentschcellars.com
Tasting room: Daily 10-6
Tasting fee: Complimentary
Wine Prices: $16-50

An understated winery where the wines are the star, with a cozy vibe, and warmly engaging hosts at the bar. This relatively new winery in the heart of the Golden Mile has amassed a trove of award winning wines, including the must-try Syrah. The enthusiastic tasting staff will keep you entertained and regale you with tales about each wine.

Try the bold Chardonnay, the plush Cab/Merlot, and especially The Chase (a blend of Cab Franc, Cab Sauv, Merlot, Petit Verdot, and Malbec). The winery offers a free bottle of Chase or free shipping with the purchase of a case.

You'll often see the friendly face of co-owner Chris visiting the tasting room, and sharing his passion for the wines. The vineyard itself is perhaps located in one of the best sites in the valley along the Golden Mile. Look for the beautifully manicured row of trees that line the drive behind the winery.

*CULMINA FAMILY ESTATE WINERY

4790 Wild Rose St, Oliver
(250)498-0789
www.culmina.ca
Tasting room: Daily 10-5 with set tasting times (hourly from 10:15 am - 4:15 pm). Reservations highly recommended via their website. Drop-ins are accommodated at tastings if room permits.
Tasting fee: From $10 pp, with $5 WWP
Wine Prices: $21-38

Head to Culmina for intentionally crafted, meticulous estate wines, at a state-of-the-art gated boutique winery seated high on the Golden Mile.

Wine geeks and

fans of premium wines will both delight in the care and attention Culmina devotes to the well tended vineyards, and inside the chic winery room (think chandelier in the tank room, and vinyl collection in the tasting room). The winery and tasting room enjoy incredible views looking towards Osoyoos.

Don Triggs was one of the founding fathers of the Okanagan wine scene, you might recognize his surname from the Jackson-Triggs brand. He sold his business interests there, retired, then was inspired to start Culmina with his family. Culmina's wines are very popular with collectors and at high-end Vancouver restaurants, and include vibrant dry Unicus (Gruner Veltliner) and Decora (Riesling), a gently-oaked Dilemma (Chardonnay), a crisp rosé that's one of the best in the valley called Saignée, elegant Bordeaux-style red called Hypothesis (Merlot, Cab Sauv, Cab Franc) that's worth laying down, and a Merlot-based red blend called R&D.

*FAIRVIEW CELLARS

989 Cellar Rd, Oliver (off Golf Course Rd)
(250)498-2211
www.fairviewcellars.ca
Tasting room: Daily 11-5
Tasting fee: Complimentary
Wine Prices: $20-120

Pull up to this rustic log cabin tasting room of BC wine pioneers, and you'll feel like you're visiting old friends. You might even be greeted at your car by a happy golden retriever.

Fairview's run by laid back, experienced winemaker and grower Bill Eggert. You'll get the sense from his wines, that he's making them from the heart, which keeps fans coming back for some of the best wines in the valley. Visiting here's an authentic and uniquely Okanagan experience.

The winery recently lost much of their Syrah crop to a hungry black bear with excellent taste (it roams into the vineyards on the hunt for ripe grapes), all part of farming next to the wild.

Must tries are their flavourful Sauvignon Blanc, and appealing reds wines including Bucket O' Blood (Syrah, Cab Sauv, Cab Franc), and cellar worthy Iconoclast Cab Sauv. Also on offer are Pinot Noir, Merlot-based Madcap, and Two Hoots Cab/Merlot. If you're lucky, they'll have an older vintage of their wine open in the tasting room for you to sample.

*GEHRINGER BROTHERS ESTATE WINERY

876 Road 8, Oliver
(250)498-3537
www.gehringerwines.ca
Tasting room: Daily 9-5:30
Tasting fee: Complimentary (Icewine tasting $2 WWP of Icewine)
Wine Prices: $11-42

This is one of the oldest family-run estates in the valley, offering a wide selection of tasty wines at great values, in particular their white wines. Because they were one of the first, they can afford to keep prices perfect for everyday enjoyment. These perpetually award-winning wines are well made and flavourful.

The brother's German heritage comes through with aromatic whites Riesling, Ehrenfelser, and Gew/Schonburger, plus others including Sauv Blanc, Chard, and Pinot Gris, and hit blend Desert Sun (Auxerrois, Chard, Riesling). For reds there's: Pinot Noir, Merlot, and Cab/Merlot, plus blend Summer Night (Pinot Noir, Cab Sauv, Merlot). Icewine lovers will enjoy the Riesling, Ehrenfelser, and Cab Franc.

GOLD HILL WINERY

3502 Fruitvale Way, Oliver (at HWY 97)
(250)495-8152
www.goldhillwinery.com
Tasting room: Daily 10-6
Tasting fee: $5 pp WWP
Wine Prices: $18-36

Strike gold at this family winery and vineyard that features bold flavours. The owners, brothers Sant and Gurbachan who moved here from India, are long time fruit growers that smartly decided to start producing their own wine with the help of consultant Philip Soo.

In the saffron yellow building, you'll find intensely aromatic whites like the Gewürztraminer and Viognier. Signature reds like the Cab Franc, Malbec, Cab/Merlot and Syrah are some of the best value red wines in the Okanagan.

The tasting bar is friendly and informal. Locals bring their friends here because they know the family is a source of grapes for other higher priced labels in the valley. Visit in the next few years and you can brag about knowing the place before they became a well known name at Vancouver and Calgary tables.

*HESTER CREEK ESTATE WINERY

877 Road 8, Oliver
(250) 498-4435 TF (866)498-4435
www.hestercreek.com
Tasting room: Daily 10-7
Restaurant: Terrafina - Daily 11:30-9
Tasting fee: Complimentary
Wine Prices: $17-45

This popular Tuscan-style hillside winery on the Golden Mile has much to offer: a large, welcoming tasting room, picnic patio area, Terrafina restaurant (reservations highly recommended), and guest suites. Hester Creek also has gorgeous views looking over the Black Sage bench. Check their website for events including live music, cooking classes, BBQs, and private food & wine pairing lessons.

Expect a good selection of well-made wines to taste at the bar, including their easy-drinking and good value Character blends available in red and white, plus Chardonnay, Trebbiano, Pinot Blanc and sweet Late Harvest Pinot Blanc, Pinot Gris, Cabernet Franc Rosé, and Cabernet Franc. They're well recog-

nized for their delicious Merlot, which is available as a reserve, and also blended with Cabernet Sauv and Cab Franc in their bold The Judge. Private tastings are available by appointment from $5-15 pp, call the winery to book.

Cozy Terrafina restaurant offers lunch and dinner, wood-fired pizzas and fresh pasta, and has a lovely vine-covered outdoor patio that feels very Italian. Reservations are required for dinner. They're open for brunch on Sundays.

The Villa has six well appointed Mediterranean-inspired view suites which include breakfast, with nightly rates ranging from $229-329/night, and $279-399 for the Sirena suite.

*INTERSECTION ESTATE WINERY

450 Road 8, Oliver (at HWY 97)
(250)498-4054
www.xwine.ca
Tasting room: Daily 11-5
Tasting fee: $5 pp WWP
Wine Prices: $19-55

Intersection is a modern winery producing some of the most terroir focused and expressive wines around. The clean lines of the tasting bar underline that a visit here is all about the juice.

The wines have a notable crystalline purity, and are incredibly well balanced on the palate. This producer is part of the new wave of Okanagan wineries that are making wine specific to special vineyard sites. Try and compare Merlot from sand versus silt, taste the difference soil can make, and appreciate the local terroir. This is definitely a place where wine nerds who delight in soil types and horizontal tastings can geek out.

The Merlots are stars, but also try their barrel ferment Viognier/Marsanne and Sauvignon Blanc, as well as the Cab Franc. Intersection is also making a bold appassimento (dried grape) style wine similar to how Italy's Amarone is made.

MAVERICK ESTATE WINERY

3974 HWY 97, Oliver
(778)437-3133
www.maverickwine.ca
Tasting room: Daily 10-5:30
Tasting fee: $3 pp WWP
Wine Prices: $17-32

Cool art gallery vibe in this bijoux tasting room, run by a family transplanted from South Africa, with a focus on thoughtful, collectable wines. Old world techniques are being used to make fruity yet elegant bottles from the Okanagan.

Care has been lavished on the wines, including an traditional method sparkling called Ella (Pinot Noir, Chardonnay), a deliciously silky Syrah, and unique fortified Syrah called Fia, Burgundian style Pinot Noir and Chardonnay, and bolder Rubeus (a blend of Syrah, Cab Sauv, Cab Franc, and Merlot). They also produce Sauv Blanc, Pinot Gris, and the enjoyable Origin (Gew, Sauv Blanc, Pinot Gris).

ROAD 13 VINEYARDS

799 Ponderosa Rd, Oliver
(250)498-8330

www.road13vineyards.com
Tasting room: Daily 10-5:30
Tasting fee: $5 pp WWP
Wine Prices: $18-75

You're in the right place if you see the stone castle; it's a relic from previous owners. These days family-run Road 13 have added a more modern glass-walled wing, and make full bodied, fruit forward wines, with some of the oldest vines in the valley.

If you love a richer style of Chardonnay, you'll love Road 13's creamy oak kissed versions. Try their Jackpot series of reserve and small lot wines, including Chard, Syrah, Cab Sauv, and Petit Verdot. Their Road 13 line has plenty of French varietals, including Marsanne, Viognier, and Chenin Blanc, plus Syrah, Syrah/Mourvedre, and Pinot Noir. They're perhaps best recognized for their Chenin in sparkling and still styles (plus a sweet late harvest). All are crowd pleasing wines, the kind you can bring to a party and everyone will enjoy.

The tasting room inside the castle is large, enjoys a view over the valley, and has a selection of wine merchandise and accessories for sale. Lounge tastings of Jackpot are available at $10 pp with the option of a charcuterie board ($25).

RUSTICO FARM & CELLARS

4444 Golden Mile Dr, Oliver
(250)498-3276
www.rusticowinery.com

Tasting room: Daily 10-6
Tasting fee: Complimentary with purchase
Wine Prices: $18-36

Visiting Rustico is like travelling back in time to a Gold Rush era cottage complete with laundry hanging on the line, winery dogs, and an Old West themed cabin that serves as the tasting room, called the Lonesome Quail Saloon (you can print an Honorary Deputy Wine Marshall certificate from their website to be deputized).

Popular with locals and visitors, their best wines often sell out early in the season, but they also offer older vintages for sale which is a treat. If you're brave sample their chili wine hot sauce. Best known for their old vine Zinfandel, Gewürztraminer, and Merlot, they also have Pinot Gris and Pinot Noir, all whimsically named.

There's an informal picnic friendly area to relax at this entertaining spot, which miraculously survived the wildfires of 2015.

*TINHORN CREEK VINEYARDS

537 Tinhorn Creek Rd, Oliver
(250)498-3743
www.tinhorn.com
Tasting room: Daily 10-6
Restaurant: Miradoro - Daily 11:30-9
Tasting fee: Complimentary
Wine Prices: $16-32

Established in 1993, this is the largest winery in the Golden Mile area, located at the top of the hill, with a generously proportioned tasting room, and plenty of amenities. The well-trained staff are experienced with accommodating larger groups. There's a great view from the tasting room and veranda overlooking the valley.

The Oldfield Series Cab Franc rosé has a devoted following, as do their Pinot Noir, Syrah, Merlot, and Cab Franc reds. For whites, check out their Chardonnay, Pinot Gris, Gew, and popular aromatic 2Bench blend (Sauv Blanc, Semillon, Chardonnay, Viognier, Muscat).

Their restaurant Mirodoro is one of the best in the area, with wall to wall windows, featuring locally sourced ingredients prepared with Mediterranean influence. Reservations are highly recommended.

Reserve and cellar tours (including wine tasting and charcuterie) can be booked in advance from $30-40 pp, and self-guided tours are also available. Check their website for events like outdoor concerts, yoga in the vineyards, and dancing lessons. The winery also offers access to the Golden Mile Trail, a favourite with hikers.

VINAMITÉ CELLARS

5381 HWY 97, Oliver
(250)498-2234
www.vinamitecellars.com
Tasting room: Daily 10-5
Tasting fee: $5 pp WWP
Wine Prices: $22-38

A delightful new family-run winery producing quality wines in a particularly welcoming art-filled wine lounge off the highway. Working together in the vineyard and producing the wine as a team, you can sense the passion behind this project. The tasting room is petite, and walking in feels like you're a welcome guest of the family.

The Lost Block Chardonnay is a winner, under a previous owner the grapes used to be blended into other wineries' labels, but they're now celebrated and bottled as a vineyard block (hence the winery's name, which was changed recently from vin-Perdu due to a trademark issue). Also available are Pinot Gris, Gamay Noir, Cab Franc, and blends Compass (Cab Sauv, Merlot, Cab Franc) and Hidden Corner (Merlot, Cab Franc).

BLACK SAGE BENCH AREA

With the windows down, the first thing you'll notice here is the sweet scent of dried sage. The rocks and sand in this area, combined with long sunny days, make it a fantastic growing zone.

The Black Sage Bench is home to several notable producers, and the perfect spot to finish a day of Oliver winetripping while taking in the sunset. Note: Covert Farms, River Stone, and Inniskillin/Jackson-Triggs are just north of the bench, but have been included in this section.

BARTIER BROTHERS

4821 Ryegrass Rd, Oliver
(250)809-5808
www.bartierbros.com
Tasting room: Daily 11-5:30
Tasting fee: $5 pp WWP
Wine Prices: $19-30

Winegrowers and winemakers, brothers Don and Michael are well known in the valley. Michael has made wine for several high profile producers (Road 13, OK Crushpad). They've started their own winery, dedicated to quality farming, and low intervention wines that are silky and balanced. Their personable new tasting room is wine country rustic, with metal cladding and shade sails.

Bartier do a small number of wines very well: Gew, Semillon, an unoaked and a richer barrel fermented Chard, and reds include Cab Franc, Syrah, and Merlot, plus their blend The Goal (Cab Franc, Merlot). They're making a serious case for growing what some think could be recognized as the Okanagan's signature grapes, Chardonnay, Syrah, and Cab Franc. Tasting fees are donated to the SPCA.

*BLACK HILLS ESTATE WINERY

4190 Black Sage Rd, Oliver
(250)498-0666
www.blackhillswinery.com
Tasting room: Daily 10-7
Restaurant: Vineyard Kitchen - Daily 11-6:30
Tasting fee: $10-50 pp for Portfolio Wine Tastings
Wine Prices: $22-52

Those seeking out a unique tasting experience should visit Black Hills, where tasting flights are served in varietally-specific stemware, guided by knowledgeable "Wine Evangelists". All this while overlooking vineyards in the heart of the Black Sage Bench. Generous two ounce pours mean tasting fees aren't waived. A luxurious experience akin to sitting poolside at a fancy hotel.

Premium wines like their big Bordeaux-style red Nota Bene are highly sought after, and the Carmenere is also a hot ticket. The Alibi Sauvignon Blanc/Semillon blend is appealing, as are the Viognier, Chardonnay, and Syrah. This winery has many shareholders, one of whom is 90210 actor Jason Priestley.

The Vineyard Kitchen serves nibbles like salads, dips, cheese, charcuterie and gourmet pizzas.

*BURROWING OWL

500 Burrowing Owl Pl, Oliver
(250)498-0620 TF (877)498-0620
www.burrowingowlwine.ca
Tasting room: Daily 10-6
Restaurant: The Sonora Room - Daily 11:30-4:30 & 5-9
Tasting fee: $3 pp
Wine Prices: $20-45

If you're going to visit just one winery in Oliver, Burrowing Owl should be it. This immensely popular estate winery helped establish BC's wine reputation with their palate friendly whites, and ripe, rich reds.

Perched overlooking the valley, enjoying awe inspiring views, the impressive building houses a tasting room and fine dining at their Sonora Room restaurant. They offer private tours through their gravity-fed winery (booked with at least 72 hours notice).

There's a dedicated following for their Pinot Noir, Merlot, Syrah, Cabernet Franc, and the Athene and Meritage red blends. Expect whites that don't shy away from full flavour (Chardonnay, Pinot Gris, and Sauvignon Blanc). Tasting fees are donated to owl conservation.

The winery has 10 luxurious suites at their Guest House, each offering a fireplace and private deck, which include breakfast, with access to a swimming pool and hot tub overlooking the vineyards. Room rates range from $169-349/night, and $469-939 for the two bedroom Meritage Suite.

INNISKILLIN OKANAGAN VINEYARDS/JACKSON-TRIGGS OKANAGAN ESTATE WINERY

7857 Tucelnuit Dr, Oliver
(250)498-4500 TF (866)455-0559
www.inniskillin.com/okanagan
www.jacksontriggswinery.com
Tasting room: Daily 10-6
Tasting fee: $2 pp
Wine Prices: $11-87

This winery, owned by the conglomerate Constellation, is located in what looks from the outside like a well manicured office park. Once you step inside, behold, it's one of the best decorated tasting bars in the valley, akin to a boutique restaurant.

You'll find a selection of small lot and reserve bottles, along with incredibly fun, storytelling staff, happy to chat about wine and make recommendations. If you have time, it's the perfect spot to do a longer tasting and food/wine pairing session at the custom bar. JT's impressively ripe reds from their famous Sun Rock vineyards on Black Sage Bench, such as the Shiraz, are a highlight, as are the Inniskillin Riesling and Cab Franc Icewines.

Seated tastings in their gorgeous tasting lounge start from $10 pp for single vineyard wines, and $15 for Icewines between 12-4 with pre-booking.

LE VIEUX PIN

5496 Black Sage Rd, Oliver
(250)498-8388
www.levieuxpin.ca
Tasting room: Daily 10:30-6:30
Tasting fee: $10 pp WWP of $30 & premium $18 pp WWP of $80
Wine Prices: $18-80

Like a little piece of Southern France. This name comes from the French for "old pine". Visit here to sample their upscale wines like the Vaila, a dry rosé made from Pinot Noir, or the Rhone-inspired Ava (Viognier, Roussanne, Marsanne) and especially the the Syrahs, which are savoury, elegant and complex sippers.

Some people think Syrah is *the* best grape for the area, so this is a wonderful spot to try single vineyard Syrah wines from different soils. They even have glass jars in the tasting room, showing the different colours and textures of earth found in their vineyards.

This is the sister winery to La Stella in Osoyoos, with the same winemaker.

MONTAKARN ESTATE WINERY

5462 Black Sage Rd,
Oliver
(250)498-7709
www.montakarn.ca
Tasting room: Daily
10-8
Tasting fee: $5 pp
WWP
Wine Prices: $14-28

Approaching though the vines, you'll spot this striking red-roofed barn winery. Here you'll find an honest farm-to-wineglass style where you'll get a sense of the heart and soul effort given to crafting wine. Winemaker Gary, who's often in the tasting room, named the winery for his wife.

This is the only place I've heard of that's pouring the grape variety Marselan, a delicious French crossing of Grenache and

Cab Sauv. Gary has quite a talent for making blends, so you'll find several here like a Sangiovese/Nebbiolo rosé, and popular red Angel Share (Malbec, Syrah, Merlot, Cab Franc).

Because this hidden gem is still under the radar, the wines offer good value compared to those of similar quality made in the area.

*SILVER SAGE WINERY

4852 Ryegrass Rd, Oliver
(250)498-0310
www.silversagewinery.com
Tasting room: Daily 10-6
Tasting fee: By donation
Wine Prices: $16-27

Silver Sage has one of the most visited winery tasting bars in the area, with guests seeking out a memorable experience. Wines are flavourful, full-bodied and all about having fun. These are wines made to pair with food, not bound by any rules of snobbery. Ask a local wine lover for their favourite tasting room and you might just hear Silver Sage, they've got a devoted following.

Whites are bursting with fruity, intense, bold flavours, like the Pinot Blanc, and "Grand Reserve" Gew fermented with wild sage plants. Reds include Merlot, and ripe Pinot Noir. Silver Sage offers a unique selection of dessert and sweet wines, notably a spicy wine called Flame, bottled with a chili pepper inside. Fruit infused sweet wines, like raspberry and peach, delight in breaking the rules.

There are three nicely appointed guest suites on site, ranging from $120-220/night.

STONEBOAT PINOT HOUSE

356 Orchard Grove Ln, Oliver
(250)498-2226
www.stoneboatvineyards.com
Tasting room: Daily 10-5:30
Tasting fee: $3 pp WWP
Wine Prices: $19-55

The Pinot specialists: think Pinotage, Pinot Noir, and Pinot Gris. If you want to know more about BC Pinot, this small, family estate winery is the perfect stop. Stoneboat has a low-key, bright and pretty room, complete with piano in the corner. Setting up the winery meant they had to remove many rocks from their vineyards, and a stoneboat is a sledge used to carry them away, hence the name.

Tasting room staff are friendly and happy to talk about the importance of Pinot family grapes. They've recently caused a stir with their fanciful, pocket book friendly "Stoned" red and white blends. There's also their immensely popular "Piano", a Prosecco-inspired Pinot Blanc sparkling, and a Pinotage, which can be a tricky grape to grow well (they're recognized as the experts in the valley).

All the wines are impeccably made, fruit driven, and nicely balanced.

*COVERT FARMS FAMILY ESTATE

300 Covert Pl, Oliver
(250)498-9463
www.covertfarms.ca
Tasting room: Daily 11-5
Tasting fee: Complimentary
Wine Prices: $17-46
Organic

Proud organic farming evangelists, with a gourmet hippy vibe. Tucked behind the hills, this large organic estate exudes bucolic charm. Chickens wander outside the rustic chic tasting room. Staff are friendly, and service is casual and unfussy. Deli/picnic items are available inside to purchase, perfect for enjoying in one

of the valley's best winery picnic spots, under a covered terrace overlooking sunny gardens.

Covert are experimenting with a blush sparkling Zin made in an ancient method, and also make the lush Odie sparkling, along with still Pinot Blanc, Viognier, and Sauv Blanc/Semillon. They're known for their reds, like the Amicitia blend (Merlot, Cab Sauv, Cab Franc, Malbec, Petit Verdot), and Zinfandel.

Book ahead for a tour in their glossy red vintage truck, to rumble through the vineyards, taste wines and snack on charcuterie, olives, and cheese, at 10:45 and 12:45 daily ($49 pp, 60-90 minutes). Or, hike the trails up to iconic Okanagan landmark the McIntyre Bluffs.

WINETRIPPING

*RIVER STONE ESTATE WINERY

143 Buchanan Dr, Oliver
(250)498-0043
www.riverstoneestatewinery.ca
Tasting room: Daily 11-6
Tasting fee: Complimentary
Wine Prices: $20-42

Make sure to visit this cozy, casual, sun-filled tasting room, where regulars are greeted by name. The winery is happily situated on top of a knoll overlooking the vineyards and gardens, and bonus: there's a friendly winery dog. But it's the wines that stand out, they're uniformly delicious, with a focus on quality at a fair price. You'll want to buy at least one of everything they have to offer.

Reds in particular have a loyal following, like the Merlot, Malbec, Cab Franc, and ageworthy Stones Throw Bordeaux-style blend. Whites include Sauvignon Blanc, Pinot Gris, and lively blend Splash (Pinot Gris, Viognier, Gewurtztraminer), and they make a tasty Malbec rosé too.

River Stone's Wine Cottage is a two bedroom charmer available from $150/night (minimum 3 nights).

OKANAGAN FALLS/SKAHA

If Oliver's the heart of wine country, then Skaha may be the soul: whether getting a glimpse of Vaseux Lake through the skyscraper Ponderosa pines, taking a moment to admire the beauty of McIntyre Bluff and Peach Cliff, or enjoying an ice cream from Tickleberry's, you'll feel it.

If travelling between Okanagan Falls and Penticton, take the eastern Skaha Lake route (Lakeside Rd) for a very special drive along the water.

BC WINE STUDIO

2434 Oliver Ranch Rd, Okanagan Falls
(250)497-8778
www.bcwinestudio.ca
Tasting room: By appointment
Tasting fee: Complimentary
Wine Prices: $17-35

By appointment only, but very happy to receive guests. A great choice for groups who want a personalized and informal experience with a longtime winemaker. Mark will open up the room for you to taste through his wines, Siren's Call. You might even get to taste barrel samples of his current projects.

Make sure to try his award winning Syrah, and one of the only wines in BC made from the zesty Austrian Gruner Veltliner grape. Several brands are made on site, including Noble Beast, Phasion, and Black Market. Before you leave, enjoy a walk through some of the valley's oldest plantings (like the thick trunked 1989 Cab Sauv), and watch the tree line to spot the hawks that nest there.

*BLUE MOUNTAIN VINEYARD & CELLARS

2385 Allendale Rd, Okanagan Falls
(250)497-8244
www.bluemountainwinery.com
Tasting room: Daily 11-5
Tasting fee: $5 pp WWP
Wine Prices: $18-40

This is one of BC's original and iconic family-owned estate wineries, growing grapes for over 40 years. Situated over Skaha Lake with pretty views of rolling vineyards and pine trees, is their beguilingly ivy-covered tasting room.

Famed for their Pinot Noir and Chardonnay, they produce some of the best traditional method bubblies in the valley, which will knock your socks off. Also on offer are Sauvignon Blanc, Pinot Blanc, Pinot Gris, and Gamay Noir.

PS: the Pinot Noirs can sell out quickly upon release, if you see some, snatch them up.

*LIQUIDITY WINES

4720 Allendale Rd,
Okanagan Falls
(778)515-5500
www.liquidity-
wines.com
Tasting room: Daily
11-6
Restaurant: Liquidity
Bistro - Daily 11-9
Tasting fee: $5 pp
WWP & $15 pp pre-
mium wines WWP 2
bottles
Wine Prices: $18-26

Pull up the winding drive to the impressive white winery building, and admire the eye-catching art pieces installed amidst the gardens. This winery enjoys on the of the best views of any in the valley on their patio overlooking Vaseux Lake, making it an ideal place to finish your tour and admire the scenery over a glass.

Wines include a crisply mineral yet creamy Chardonnay, Riesling, Viognier, and Pinot Gris, and smooth lush reds, like the standout Pinot Noir, Merlot, and Dividend blend (Cab Sauv/Cab Franc) poured by the consummate professionals behind the bar. VIP tastings can be booked for 2-4 people ($49-98) including matching charcuterie.

The bistro is a great spot to relax in, filled with art, serving wine country cuisine like beef tenderloin with mushroom and pistachio, or Char with fennel salad.

*MEYER FAMILY VINEYARDS

4287 McLean Creek Rd, Okanagan Falls
(250)497-8553
www.mfvwines.com
Tasting room: Daily 10-5
Tasting fee: Complimentary-
$5 pp for deluxe tasting
Wine Prices: $18-40

A must-do for Pinot Noir hounds, Meyer's widely considered one of the best Pinot producers in the country for a reason. A low lying series of red buildings surround their low key but classy tasting room.

Whites available include Chardonnay, Riesling, Gewurztraminer, and a Chardonnay/PN bubbly.

Try a flight of their site-specific Pinots, or, enjoy a custom tasting in their garden cabana from $25-35 pp (book at least 24 hours ahead). Meyer's juicy, full-flavoured, yet balanced wines prove their focused strategy is a major success.

NIGHTHAWK VINEYARDS

2735 Green Lake Road, Okanagan Falls
(250)497-8874
www.nighthawkvineyards.com

Tasting room: Daily 10-5
Tasting fee: By donation
Wine Prices: $20-32

Drive up the ridge from See Ya Later, stopping to admire the jade-hued waters of Green Lake before arriving at Nighthawk's log cottage. They've been growing grapes for several years, and are proud to welcome you to their newly opened farm gate winery. A nighthawk is a nocturnal bird recognized by their distinctive cry.

On offer are Gewürztraminer, a particularly good example, plus Viognier, Merlot, Cab Sauv and an impressive Syrah. They'll be releasing their Chardonnay and Pinot Noir in Autumn of 2016.

Take it all in from a seat on their patio or lawn, and keep an eye out for the deer that like to roam this area. Tasting fees are donated to the Nature Trust of BC.

NOBLE RIDGE VINEYARD & WINERY

2320 Oliver Ranch Rd, Okanagan Falls
(250)497-7945
www.nobleridge.com
Tasting room: Daily 10-5
Tasting fee: $5 pp WWP
Wine Prices: $20-55

Stop to admire the interestingly shaped vines on the way in to this petite and homey family-owned winery. Outside in the vineyard, shard eyed winetrippers will spot their sculptural double canopy vines.

This under the radar hidden gem is producing excellent quality wines. Make sure to try their Champagne-inspired sparkling called The One, which is laid down for several years to become richly toasty. They're known for their Chardonnay, and do a delicious red Meritage blend. The Reserve and King's Ransom Pinot Noir are standouts.

There's a pretty picnic area, with cheese, charcuterie, olive and nuts available for purchase.

SEE YA LATER RANCH

2575 Green Lake Rd, Okanagan Falls
(250)497-8267
www.sylranch.com
Tasting room: Daily 10-6
Restaurant: See Ya Later Restaurant - Thurs-Mon 12-3
Tasting fee: $2 pp
Wine Prices: $14-23

Worth the winding drive from OK Falls up the hill, SYL is an approachable winery with generous selection of tasty and affordable wines. The winery's themed after an old rancher who owned the property, and his beloved pet dogs. You'll notice the original

1930's barn which still hosts events, as you pull up the drive. It's a popular stop, and can fill with large groups in high season.

Friendly tasting room staff will pour from a selection, including their Gewürztraminer, one of the grapes they're best known for, and reds, like Pinot Noir, the Rover (Shiraz, Viognier), or Major's Block (Merlot, Shiraz, Cab Sauv, Zinfandel). Their Sparkling Brut made in the traditional method is also popular.

There's a lunch restaurant on site, or enjoy the view from their east facing patio, which is open from 12-4. Keep an eye out for deer in the parking lot. Tasting fees are donated to the SPCA. Make sure to stop at Nighthawk Vineyards up the road.

*SYNCHROMESH WINES

4220 McLean Creek Rd, Okanagan Falls
(250)535-1558
www.synchromeshwines.ca
Tasting room: Daily 11-5
Tasting fee: Complimentary
Wine Prices: $19-50

A destination of pilgrimage for Riesling lovers, their many versions range to off-dry, full of intense mineral and lime flavours, with plenty of acidity.

Beware, these small-lot wines are in very high demand. Synchromesh may sell out early in the season and close their tasting room thereafter, so check their website to confirm before visiting (they closed as of August for the 2016 season).

This is the kind of winery you set aside some time to enjoy. The tasting room, which is set in a small glass walled building, is like sitting at the long table of a hip café. You'll soon understand their labour of love philosophy, farming on their rocky home site, and working with trusted

growers to craft site-specific Rieslings like the Thorny Vines or Storm Haven. They're also generating buzz for their excellent Cab Franc, and Tertre Rouge blend of Cab Franc/Merlot. If you miss out, do keep an eye out on restaurant wine lists for them.

*WILD GOOSE VINEYARDS & WINERY

2145 Sun Valley Way, Okanagan Falls
(250)497-8919
www.wildgoosewinery.com
Tasting room: Daily 10-7
Restaurant: Smoke & Oak Bistro - Daily 12-7

Tasting fee: Complimentary-$3 pp WWP
Wine Prices: $16-32

This bright and welcoming spot is a must-visit for white wine lovers who enjoy a smooth style with some sweetness, and lots of flavour in their glass. Wild Goose wines are well appreciated by locals and the pricing is a steal for the value.

Aromatic blend Autumn Gold (Pinot Blanc, Gew, Riesling) is a particular favourite, along with Riesling, Gew, Pinot Blanc, and Pinot Gris. If you enjoy sweet wines make sure you try their Botrytis Riesling. For reds, there's Merlot, and bold Red Horizon Meritage (Merlot, Cab Sauv, Petit Verdot), plus Port-inspired Black Brant made from Merlot and Petit Verdot.

Their wines pair perfectly with the southern BBQ served at their casual Smoke & Oak Bistro, which looks out onto their vines and Peach Cliff hills, and often features live music. Vine cuttings and barrel staves are used in their Tennessee smoker.

PENTICTON/NARAMATA

Penticton's a lively town, nicely situated between Skaha and Okanagan Lakes and equidistant between Osoyoos and Kelowna. Plenty of restaurants and hotels make it a great home base for exploring the valley from.

Scenic Naramata Bench is just minutes away, densely packed with wineries, ideal for a one day wine trip. It's also increasingly popular with cyclists doing the Kettle Valley trail who finish their day by stopping in for refreshments.

PENTICTON

If you're in town on a Saturday, make sure to check out the farmer's market, it's really something special, with all kinds of baked goods, fresh garden produce, and even local wineries in attendance.

WINETRIPPING

Painted Rock is included in this sub-section, but you'll find the winery just south of Penticton; consider including a stop here before or after your tour of Okanagan Falls wineries.

*PAINTED ROCK ESTATE WINERY

400 Smythe Dr, Penticton
(250)493-6809
www.paintedrock.ca
Tasting room: 11-5:30
Tasting fee: $10 pp WWP
Wine Prices: $22-48

An iconic winery with impressive modernist tasting room that looks straight out of Dwell Magazine, which enjoys an incredible view over Skaha Lake. Painted Rock are busy putting BC on the map, with international wine critics singing their praises.

They're best known for their structured, ageable reds like the Red Icon (Merlot, Cab Franc, Malbec, Petit Verdot, Cab Sauv), and smooth Merlot, Syrah, and Cabernet Sauvignon. They also produce Chardonnay, and a rosé from their six red varietals.

Their patio is a lovely place to enjoy a glass of wine paired with cheese/charcuterie, or just to admire the view. Check their website for exclusive winery dinners featuring some of the best chefs in the valley.

TIME WINERY - COMING EARLY 2017

250 Winnipeg St, Penticton
(250)494-8828
www.timewinery.com
Tasting room: Daily 11-8
Restaurant: Bistro TBD
Tasting fee: TBD
Wine Prices: $16-35

This urban winery is currently under construction, a reimagining of the classic Penman Theatre in downtown Penticton, and it's one to watch for in early 2017.

You'll be able to taste Time wines including the impressive Meritage white (Sauv Blanc, Semillon), Syrah, and Cab Franc, plus premium series McWatters Collection Chardonnay and red Meritage wines from the tasting lounge, host events, and even grab a bite to eat.

The McWatters family, veterans of the BC wine scene, also own the Evolve Cellars brand winery in Summerland, a very nice spot to stop for lunch looking over the water and enjoy well made wines at fair prices (20623 McDougald Rd, 778-516-7728).

NARAMATA BENCH

BELLA WINES

4320 Gulch Rd, Naramata
(778)996-1829
www.bellawines.ca
Tasting room: Thurs-Sun 12-5
Tasting fee: $5 pp WWP
Wine Prices: $25-55

Follow Naramata trail to the end of the bench for some of the best sparkling wines made in BC.

Focused on Chardonnay and Gamay, this winery works exclusively on bubbly. Bella is all about site specific, minimal intervention wines, and they're purists, so their wines are for lovers of dry bubblies in the style of grower Champagne.

The tasting room closes when the winery sells out of wine, which can happen mid-summer (closed as of August in 2016. Re-opening for tasting May long weekend 2017). Picnics are welcome on their patio.

DAYDREAMER WINES

1305 Smethurst Rd, Naramata
(778)514-0026
www.daydreamerwines.ca
Tasting room: Daily 11:30-5:30
Tasting fee: Complimentary-$5 pp WWP
Wine Prices: $20-35

A bijoux winery run by a husband and wife team (he's a Master of Wine). Their little blue wine shack has recently opened for tastings.

Bone dry terroir-focused Riesling, pure and steely, is a standout. There's also Pinot Gris, Jay Pinot Noir, a rosé (Pinot Noir, Syrah, Merlot), Amelia (Syrah, Viognier), Jasper (Merlot, Cab

Franc), and the premium line Marcus Ansems Signature Chard and Shiraz.

Daydreamer is a perfect stop for wine lovers who want a glimpse of ultra-small production, low intervention, hand crafted wines.

*DEEP ROOTS VINEYARD

884 Tillar Rd, Naramata
(250)460-2390
www.deeprootswinery.com
Tasting room: Daily 11-5:30
Tasting fee: $5 pp WWP
Wine Prices: $19-40

A new winery launched by longtime farmers that's making serious waves, Deep Roots' wines will impress. Their rustic, woodsy, board and batten tasting room, with warmly friendly staff, might remind you a little of Hobbiton.

Wines are full-bodied and food-friendly, especially their award-winning Syrah, Merlot, and Chardonnay. Whites also include Pinot Gris, Sauvignon Blanc, and for reds Cab Franc, Malbec, and Gamay.

*JOIEFARM WINERY

2825 Naramata Rd, Naramata
(250)496-0092
www.joiefarm.com
Tasting room: Daily 10-5

Restaurant: Picnique - Daily 11:30-4:30
Tasting fee: $5 pp WWP
Wine Prices: $18-40

Take a little bit of pastoral veggie garden farm, roaming chickens, and a hint of French countryside, and you might just get something like JoieFarm.

They have the perfect spot for lunch, Picnique, ideal for looking over the orchard and lake while munching on wood-fired pizza from their outdoor oven or a delicious ice-cream sandwich.

In the casual tasting room, seek out the Pinot Noir, Alsatian-inspired Noble Blend (Gew, Riesling, Pinot Auxerrois, Pinot Blanc, Muscat, Schoenberger), and always save room for their Family Reserve Chard and Gew. Other wines produced include Gamay, Viognier, Riesling and a pink bubbly called Plein de Vie (Pinot Noir, Pinot Meunier, Chardonnay).

*LA FRENZ WINERY

1525 Randolph Rd, Penticton
(250)492-6690
www.lafrenzwinery.com
Tasting room: Daily 10-5
Tasting fee: $5-10 pp WWP
Wine Prices: $20-45

Anchoring the Naramata Bench is one of the valley's best wineries, and a perpetual award winner. La Frenz is crafting some seriously good wine, like their intense Alexandria (a blend of Muscats), and Grand Total Reserve, a big Bordeaux style red.

Other whites include Viognier, Chardonnay, Semillon, Riesling, and Sauvignon Blanc. Reds include Pinot Noir, Malbec, Merlot, Shiraz, and Cab Sauv. They also offer a trio of fortifieds, including a Muscat inspired by Aussie stickies, and a Port-inspired tawny and robust vintage style for laying down. The tasting room has understated elegance, and their deck is a delightful place to enjoy a glass of wine. Reservations highly recommended for tastings.

LAKE BREEZE VINEYARDS

930 Sammet Rd, Naramata
(250)496-5659
www.lakebreeze.ca

Tasting room: Daily 10:30-5:30
Restaurant: The Patio - Daily 11:30-3:30
Tasting fee: $3 pp WWP
Wine Prices: $19-50

A little slice of Tuscany, with a pretty patio full of comfy café chairs to enjoy lunch, Lake Breeze's lively tasting room is where regulars and tourists alike stop for well made and well priced wines.

There's a broad selection to choose from, for whites: Riesling, Ehrenfelser, Semillon, Sauv Blanc, Pinot Blanc, and Pinot Gris, and unique blend The Spice Jar (Gew, Ehrenfelser, Schonburger, Viongier). Reds include Pinot Noir, Pinotage, Merlot, and Syrah, plus blends Tempest (Merlot, Malbec, Cab Franc, Cab Sauv, Petit Verdot) and Meritage (Merlot, Cab Franc, Cab Sauv, Malbec).

They've recently constructed a private room for the tasting of a the McIntyre line of premium wines available exclusively at the winery. The top notch Patio restaurant is one of the best in the area, and features seasonally inspired fare like portobello carpaccio, organic local greens with pecans and goat's cheese, and cioppino.

LAUGHING STOCK VINEYARDS

1548 Naramata Rd, Penticton
(250)493-8466
www.laughingstock.ca
Tasting room: By appointment Daily 11-4:30
Tasting fee: $10 pp WWP
Wine Prices: $20-40

WINETRIPPING

By appointment only. Call ahead to arrange a personalized guided tasting. This premium producer has amassed a dedicated following with their strong emphasis on craft and quality. Perched on the top of the hill, this winery is a worthwhile stop.

The fruit comes from their vineyards on the Naramata Bench and in Osoyoos. The flagship red is Portfolio (Merlot, Cab Sauv, Cab Franc, Malbec, Petit Verdot), aged in French oak, and they also produce a Syrah, Pinot Noir, and Blind Trust blend (the contents of which are listed underneath the bottle capsule). Whites include Viognier, Pinot Gris, Chardonnay, white Blind Trust, and the Amphora wild ferment Viognier/Roussanne made with skin contact. Their Winemaker Residence rental is available to members from $3,800/week.

LITTLE ENGINE WINES

851 Naramata Rd, Penticton
(250)493-0033
www.littleenginewines.com
Tasting room: Daily 11-5
Tasting fee: Silver $5 pp, Gold $10 pp WWP of tier wine
Wine Prices: $22-55

This new winery has a chic and thoughtfully designed tasting room, with white and barn board tasting bar.

Little Engine has launched with a quality focused portfolio of Chardonnay, Sauvignon Blanc, rosé (Pinot Noir, Merlot), Merlot, and Pinot Noir, made by one of the best winemakers in the valley (formerly of La Frenz). The Chardonnay and Pinot are highlights.

Private barrel room tastings hosted by an owner or the wine-maker with paired local cheeses are $40 pp (book ahead).

MARICHEL VINEYARD & WINERY

1016 Littlejohn Rd, Naramata
(250)496-4133
www.marichel.ca
Tasting room: Daily 11-5
Tasting fee: $2 pp WWP
Wine Prices: $20-48

This is really a tiny jewel of a winery. Visiting the tasting room is like stepping into a country kitchen with shared table, and there's also a small leafy deck looking out on the lake.

They don't have a wide selection, but excel at their chosen grapes: Viognier, and Syrah. The Syrah is available in several iterations, including a rosé.

Expect a personable, personalized, and leisurely tasting experience with time to talk about the wines. If the room's not open, just call and someone should be able to come in from the vineyard nearby for you.

MOCOJO WINERY

1202 Gawne Rd, Naramata
(778)931-0265
www.mocojowines.com
Tasting room: Daily 11-5
Tasting fee: Complimentary
Wine Prices: $18-24

A newer addition to Naramata, this is a family operation of former rose growers, so you know they can farm. The vines were planted over 20 years ago. The tasting room has a folksy, friendly vibe, and there's an idyllic sunny patio to enjoy. The winery's named after the the family's three children.

Wines are well balanced and smooth, with good flavour and appealing price points. They include Viognier, Gew, enjoyable Marechal Foch, Malbec, and Merlot, and a juicy Long Stem Rosé.

MORAINE ESTATE WINERY

1865 Naramata Rd, Penticton
(250)460-1836
www.morainewinery.com
Tasting room: Daily 10-7

Tasting fee: $5 pp WWP
Wine Prices: $17-35

Named for the glacial soil, lovers of terroir should stop in here. Well versed tasting staff create a special experience, with lots of stories about the vines and wines. Kiwi winemaker Jacq mastered her trade in Central Otago.

They have a thoroughly enjoyable menu to taste you through, especially their site specific Riesling and Pinot Noir, which I think is some of the best around. There's an excellent Gew, plus Chard, Pinot Gris, Viognier, Malbec, Syrah, and an impressive Cab Franc/Merlot Icewine called Twin Peaks.

Picnics welcome on the lawn, or enjoy a glass on their deck.

NICHOL VINEYARD

1285 Smethurst Rd, Naramata
(250)496-5962
www.nicholvineyard.com
Tasting room: Daily 11-5
Tasting fee: $3 pp WWP
Wine Prices: $22-40

A well regarded producer with a fervent following, Nichol focuses on terroir and biodynamic growing.

The wines here are just delicious, especially their dusky pink hued Pinot Gris, and Syrah, making it worth the drive. They also make Cab Franc, Pinot Noir, and 'Nine Mile' Red (Pinot Noir, St. Laurent). Ask about the local bear, who I hear has a taste for butter from the deck fridge. If the winery is sold out, be sure to look out for their wines on restaurant wine lists.

Nichol's one of the furthest down the bench from Penticton, so a good place to start a day of winetripping, along with Bella. There's Kettle Valley trail access across the street.

*POPLAR GROVE WINERY

425 Middle Bench Rd N, Penticton
(250)493-9463
www.poplargrove.ca
Tasting room: Daily 10-9
Restaurant: The Vanilla Pod - Daily
11:30-4 & 5-late
Tasting fee: $5 pp WWP
Wine Prices: $17-43

The most impressive tasting room on Naramata's bench belongs to Poplar Grove, its bright, open space enhanced by the wall of windows looking over Penticton below, and featuring uniquely horseshoe shaped 'tasting pods' to gather at. Service is polished and enjoyable.

Specialties include Merlot, Syrah, Cab Franc, and Chardonnay, sourced from key sites throughout the Okanagan and Similkameen. They also do Viognier, Pinot Gris, and a popular rosé called BDN. Red blends on offer are Legacy (Merlot, Malbec, Cab Sauv, Cab Franc), and Benchmark (Merlot, Malbec, Cab Franc).

A great first stop for your tour of the bench or last spot as they have extended hours in high season, they also offer one of the nicest picnic spots around. Poplar Grove have the same ownership as Monster Vineyards down the lane, which offers affordable and fruit-forward wines.

The Vanilla Pod restaurant has the same commanding views as the tasting room, offers lunch and dinner focusing on seasonal ingredients, and serves Poplar Grove and Monster wines.

TERRAVISTA VINEYARDS

1853 Sutherland Rd, Penticton
(778)476-6011
www.terravistavineyards.com
Tasting room: Daily 12-5
Tasting fee: $3 pp WWP
Wine Prices: $19-25

A small estate winery focusing exclusively on a unique stable of white grapes, a study in winemaking technique. The Figaro is a blend of Rhone Valley varietals Marsanne, Roussanne, and Viognier, and Fandango is a blend of Spanish grapes Albarino and Verdejo. There's also a zesty 100% Albarino, and satiny Viognier.

Pouring from their modern concrete crushpad, winemaker Senka (who along with her husband, was a founder of Black Hills) is absolutely passionate about her wines, and happy to talk you through an interesting tasting. Wines have personality, and a

silky texture in common. Don't forget to say 'hi' to the friendly winery dog who'll likely greet you with a wagging tail.

VAN WESTEN VINEYARDS

2800A Aikins Loop, Naramata
(250)496-0067
www.vanwestenvineyards.com
Tasting room: Daily 11-5
Tasting fee: $3 pp WWP
Wine Prices: $20-50

From a family of orchardists and longtime Naramata farmers comes this iconoclast producer just down the lane from Joie-Farm. The tasting room has a garagiste vibe, being housed in an old fruit packing warehouse (they're the largest cherry grower on the bench), and you'll likely meet winemaker Rob van Westen inside.

Whites are full flavoured and bodied with some sweetness, with names like Vivacious, and Vicicle. The big, bold reds can pack a punch, and many are best suited to laying down for a while (perfect for pulling out a couple of years down the road to remember your visit): there's V (Merlot, Cab Franc, Malbec, Cab Sauv, Petit Verdot), Voluptuous (Merlot, Cab Franc), and Vulture, a Cab Franc, among others. Tasting fees are donated to the Children's Hospital.

SUMMERLAND/PEACHLAND

Summerland has several noteworthy niche producers scattered in the rolling hills, making for a full day of winetripping. Nearby Peachland has a pretty lakeside boardwalk with cafés and restaurants, the perfect spot to grab breakfast or lunch.

PEACHLAND

HAINLE VINEYARDS & DEEP CREEK WINE ESTATE

5355 Trepanier Bench Rd, Peachland
(250)212-5944
www.hainle.com
Tasting room: Daily 11-5

Tasting fee: $5 pp WWP
Wine Prices: $25-100+
Organic

This is one of the only wineries in Peachland, but it's well worth a visit. Winemaker and owner Walter is making some truly delicious wines in a low intervention style with very few to no additives, using historical techniques, and makes for an engaging host. Set in a wood cottage, the rough hewn tasting room is something out of a Bavarian film set.

The wines, including Cab Franc, Viognier, Pinot Noir, and Icewines will impress. The Grand Reserve Red blend (Merlot, Cab Sauv, Cab Franc, Pinot Noir, Gamay, Baco Noir) is a crowd-pleaser. The wines are released with more age on them than at most producers, which will appeal to fans of old world style wines. The tasting room often has older vintages open to sample, a welcome treat.

FITZPATRICK FAMILY VINEYARDS - COMING LATE 2016

697 HWY 97S, Peachland
(250)878-5430
www.fitzwine.com
Tasting room: Daily 10-6
Restaurant: Anticipated opening June 2017
Tasting fee: TBD
Wine Prices: $19-33

Fitz represents a complete overhaul of Greata Ranch, anticipated to open to the public in October 2016, on a historic property that was one of the area's earliest orchards. The site is
perched directly over the lake and promises to have impeccable
views. The winery has a sparkling wine focus (caves below the
tasting room will hold 120,000 bottles of traditional method bubbly), along with still Chardonnay, Pinot Blanc, Ehrenfelser, and
Gew.

Their restaurant is anticipated to open in June 2017, with
wood-fired pizza and gourmet salads.

SUMMERLAND

Head up into the hills of Summerland which are chock-a-block with hidden gem wineries. This is a hot spot for organic growers.

GIANT HEAD ESTATE WINERY

4307 Gartrell Rd, Summerland
(250)460-0749
www.giantheadwinery.com
Tasting room: Daily 11-5
Tasting fee: $10 pp WWP
Wine Prices: $21-28

Set below Giant's Head Mountain is this newer estate winery run by a husband and wife team. She is mistress of vines, having sought out the best stock throughout the valley, and he makes the wines with a laser like focus on quality. An iconoclast and per-

fectionist, he's handcrafting their small lot wines, a real winemaker's winemaker (Tom Di Bello is consulting).

Look out for an excellent Merlot, plus Pinot Noir, a bubbly Blanc de Noir (Pinot Noir), along with Gew, and a frizzante Merlot rosé.

The tasting room has a craftsman vibe, with handmade wooden shelves and wine racks.

*OKANAGAN CRUSH PAD

16576 Fosbery Rd, Summerland
(250)494-4445
www.okanagancrushpad.com
Tasting room: Daily 10:30-5:30
Tasting fee: $5 pp WWP
Wine Prices: $16-55
Organic

This is a landmark BC winery not to miss: this premium producer is setting the pace. Get a peek into a fully functioning custom crush facility, and prepare to ogle their prominent concrete egg fermenters as you taste in this bright, modernist space.

Their wines are uniformly tasty and refreshing. Haywire's wines include a lively bestselling sparkling called 'The Bub', Chardonnay, Gamay, and a delicious Pinot Noir, plus an amphora fermented orange wine made from Pinot Gris called "Wild Ferment". Narrative series wines Riesling, and Syrah are standouts. Their in-house Narrative Gin is distilled from wine.

OK Crushpad's custom crush facilities have incubated several winery projects, among them Bartier Brothers and Bella. They also sponsor the annual Okanagan Wine Campus, the lucky recipient getting to produce their own custom wine (in support of wine education scholarships), which you might see for sale in the tasting room.

*SAGE HILLS ESTATE VINEYARD & WINERY

18555 Matsu Dr, Summerland
(250)276-4344
www.sagehillswine.com
Tasting room: Daily 11-5
Tasting fee: $10-20 pp WWP
Wine Prices: $25-56 per bottle
Organic

Like visiting a show home perched over the hills, the tasting room here is a gorgeous seated bar circling the pouring area, with lake views.

Prepare for a leisurely, debonaire tasting. You may be served by Rick, the owner, a passionate believer in sustainable farming, who'll regale you with stories about their low cropping process, or earth friendly initiatives such as Salmon-Safe, or be joined in the tasting room by winemaker Tom Di Bello (formerly of Burrowing Owl).

The wines are impeccable, the Pinot Noir and Gewurz being standouts, along with Syrah (also a rosé Syrah, and a sweet fortified called AFT), Pinot Gris, Rhymes With Orange (an orange wine made from Pinot Gris), and dry bubbly Brut Sauvage.

SAXON ESTATE WINERY

9819 Lumsden Ave, Summerland
(250)494-0311
www.saxonwinery.com
Tasting room: Daily 10-5
Tasting fee: $5 pp WWP
Wine Prices: $20-27
Organic

A tiny little winery tucked back into the Summerland hills. Pull up past ancient trees lining the drive and pop into the tasting room to enjoy these organically grown wines.

When you taste these them, you'll see why they're such a well-respected insider secret. Smooth, rounded, well-balanced, with plenty of flavour. They make Pinot Grigio, Gew, Pinot Noir, and Four Play a red blend (Leon Millot, Pinot Noir, Merlot), along with English Rosé, a nod to owner Jayne's heritage. The wine-maker is Tom Di Bello.

*SILKSCARF WINERY

4917 Gartrell Rd, Summerland
(250)494-7455
www.silkw.net
Tasting room: Daily 10-5:30
Tasting fee: $3 pp WWP
Wine Prices: $21-33

An insider favourite, this tiny family run winery (who learned winemaking in their native Israel), has a modest tasting room a little like a small gallery, featuring silky and smooth wines with some sweetness, and delightful reds with reduced use of additives. These are purists making some of the region's nicest wines.

Whites include Viognier, Chardonnay, Riesling/Muscat, Roussanne/Viognier, and Alsatian-inspired Ensemble (Gew, Pinot Gris, Riesling). Reds include Merlot, Pinot Noir, Shiraz/Viognier, and standout Ensemble Cab Franc. They also produce a Malbec/Merlot rosé called Saignee.

*SUMAC RIDGE ESTATE WINERY

17403 HWY 97, Summerland
(250)494-0451
www.sumacridge.com
Tasting room: Daily 10-6
Tasting fee: $2 pp
Wine Prices: $13-31

Owned by one of the largest wine companies in Canada, you might be surprised at how warm and welcoming this spot is. The particularly knowledgable and tenured tasting room staff have a newly renovated space to entertain you in, gold mosaics and all.

Three brands are poured at the bar: Black Sage Vineyards for big, well-oaked reds grown in a hot spot on the Black Sage Bench (bold red fans will love varietal Cab

Franc, Merlot, Cab Sauv, Shiraz, Zinfandel, and Port-style Pipe); Steller's Jay, one of BC's best sparkling brands, producing traditional method bubblies which are a steal for the quality (including Champagne-inspired classics, plus sparkling Shiraz and Gewurz); and Sumac Ridge estate wines (dry unoaked whites like Pinot Grigio, Sauv Blanc, and Chardonnay, plus easygoing reds like Merlot, Shiraz, Pinot Noir, and Cab/Merlot).

Tours of the sparkling cellar and private wine & cheese paired tastings come recommended, or build a picnic from their deli fridge. Tasting fees are donated to Summerland Food Bank.

SUMMERGATE WINERY

11612 Morrow Ave, Summerland
(250)583-9973
www.summergate.ca
Tasting room: Daily 10-6
Tasting fee: Complimentary
Wine Prices: $20-50
Organic

Tucked away from other wineries is this little delight. Passionate winegrower Gillian crafts wines that are truly delicious, pure and simple. You can tell she truly cares about the land. The tasting room has a summer cottage vibe, with roaming chickens, and picnics welcome.

For now it's white wines only, with red in the pipeline. But in their favour is one of the best Rieslings around. Try their sweet 'ice'-style wine called Moonlight Frost and learn a little about how this wine's picked in freezing temperatures. They also make aromatic Kerner, and Muscat Ottonel, along with a frizzante Moscato.

TH WINES

#1 - 9576 Cedar Ave, Summerland
(250)494-8334
www.thwines.com
Tasting room: Daily 11-5
Tasting fee: $5 pp WWP
Wine Prices: $23-35

The industrial area with no vines in sight might have you thinking you're in the wrong place, but inside you'll find a cool garagiste room featuring live-edge wood bar, mason jars, and hand crafted wines popular with somms and wine lovers alike.

Tyler buys small lots of the best grapes he can find to make his sought-after wines, including Cab Franc, Viognier, Riesling, Cab Merlot blends, and Pinot Noir.

THORNHAVEN ESTATES WINERY

6816 Andrew Ave, Summerland
(250)494-7778
www.thornhaven.com
Tasting room: Daily 10-5
Tasting fee: Complimentary
Wine Prices: $15-27

Pulling up to this appealing Santa Fe style building perched over a little vine-clad valley, the red deck umbrellas beckon you in to the relaxed tasting area.

Thornhaven offers one of the broadest menu of tasting selections you'll find; they're best known for their Gewürztraminer but there's definitely something for everyone on their extensive list, poured patiently by friendly staff (including Merlot, Pinot Noir, Pinot Meunier, Orange Muscat, Chard, Pinot Gris, Riesling, and Sauv Blanc, plus bubbles, and dessert wine).

KELOWNA

This is the largest city in the Okanagan, divided in this guide into two sub-regions: West Kelowna (also known as Westbank), and across the bridge, Kelowna (or East Kelowna).

WEST KELOWNA (WESTBANK)

Wineries here include some of the most iconic in the valley, such as Mission Hill and Quail's Gate, along with tiny specialist gems.

INDIGENOUS WORLD WINERY

2218 Horizon Drive E, West Kelowna
(250)769-2824

www.indigenousworldwinery.com
Tasting room: Daily 10-7
Restaurant: Red Fox Club - Daily 11:30-8
Tasting fee: $5 pp WWP
Wine Prices: $15-35

One of the newest wineries in the Okanagan, owned by the Westbank First Nation. Their winemaker is Jason Parkes (The Hatch).

Already, IWW has made a strong start, winning all sorts of awards for their wines. Whites include Chard, Gew, and Hee-Hee-Tel-Kin blend of Viognier, Ehenfelser, and Gew (the name comes from the Okanagan Syilx for an antlered alpine stag). Full bodied reds like the winning Hee-Hee-Tel-Kin (Cab Franc, Merlot), Simo Small Lot Cab/Merlot/Cab blend, Pinot Noir, and Merlot should be snatched up.

Their Red Fox Club restaurant serves tasty aboriginal inspired cuisine for lunch and dinner, with great views from their patio.

*MISSION HILL FAMILY ESTATE WINERY

1730 Mission Hill Rd, West Kelow-na
(250)768-7611
www.missionhillwinery.com
Tasting room: Daily 9:30-7
Restaurant: The Terrace - Daily 11:30-3 & 5-9
Tasting fee: $8 pp WWP of 2 bottles
Wine Prices: $12-100+

The grandaddy of BC wineries, this producer is utterly iconic. Yes, you should definitely visit to goggle at the buildings, the art, the substantial cellar, and especially the view over Okanagan Lake.

Their tasting bar has a good selection, usually five different options each of well-made white and red wines. The Martin's Lane series is particularly good, and the Legacy series includes groundbreaking wines such as bold red blend Oculus (one of the first ultra-premium priced wines produced in BC), and rich Chardonnay Perpetua.

The winery has a wonderful terrace restaurant overlooking the lake that serves lunch and dinner, and a grassy theatre which hosts top tier concerts and plays.

Advance reservations are required for weekend tours and tastings, as it gets very busy here in high season. Book their 60 minute Reserve tour to check out their impressive barrel vaulted cellar ($15 pp), or 2 hour Vineyard Lunch & Tour to see it all plus enjoy a vineyard luncheon ($99 pp). Mission Hill also owns CedarCreek and CheckMate wineries.

OFF THE GRID ORGANIC WINERY

3623 Glencoe Rd, West Kelowna
(778)754-7562
www.offthegridorganicwinery.com
Tasting room: Daily 10-6
Tasting fee: $4 pp WWP
Wine Prices: $17-22
Organic

Such a cute little spot, a breath of fresh air after you've visited some of the monumental wineries in the area. This winery is run by a family that's farmed in the Okanagan for the past 100 years. The tasting room is built from straw bales, and pygmy goats roam the winery (check them out on the green roof).

Their easy drinking wines include a Pinot Gris, Gew, unoaked Chard, and the Unplugged Red (Merlot, Cab Sauv, Syrah).

A sweet spot to pull up a chair and have a picnic is right next to the tasting room, with a view of Okanagan Lake and Mission Hill, and there's a stocked deli cooler. Visit the sheep, heritage chickens, and turkeys, and watch those goats come running when you offer them a winery-supplied treat.

*QUAIL'S GATE ESTATE WINERY

3303 Boucherie Rd, West Kelowna
(250)769-4451
www.quailsgate.com
Tasting room: Daily 9:30-8
Restaurant: Old Vines - Daily 11-9:30
Tasting fee: Complimentary-$5 WWP of 2 bottles
Wine Prices: $17-61

A historic property farmed by the family since 1956, with a classy low-slung post and beam winery building overlooking the lake, surrounded by patios and gardens.

Best known for their Pinot Noir and Chardonnay in particular, plus Chenin Blanc, Old Vines Marechal Foch, and their standout premium Stewart Family Reserve line of wines. Dessert wine lovers can also pick up Riesling Icewine, botrytised Optima, and a Port-style Foch.

Tours are run daily at 11-1-3-5, and will give you a chance to see the oldest home in the area, Allison House, built in 1873.

The lovely Old Vines restaurant has a nice lake view, a perfect spot to relax and enjoy a special meal. Quail's Gate has two large, well-appointed lake front rentals, The Lake House, and The Nest, from $405-838/night.

ROLLINGDALE WINERY

2306 Hayman Rd, West Kelowna
(250)769-9224
www.rollingdale.ca
Tasting room: Daily 10-6
Tasting fee: $4-$13 pp WWP
Wine Prices: $14-100+
Organic

This small operation produces organic wines, served from their quonset hut (a rounded metal-roofed utility building) tasting room that also houses their winemaking area.

Rollingdale is a great stop especially if you want to try Icewines, as they make a variety of sweet wines including from Pinot Gris, Pinot Blanc, Chard, Marechal Foch, and Cab Sauv. They also make table wines from Pinot Blanc, Gew, Chard, Marechal Foch, and Cab Sauv.

THE HATCH WINES

3225 Boucherie Rd, West Kelowna
(778)755-6013
www.thehatchwines.com
Tasting room: Daily 10-8
Tasting fee: $5-10 pp WWP
Wine Prices: $15-55

A quirky and hip new winery featuring irreverent graphic designs paired with small lot wines of grapes bought from all over the valley. A barn wood clad tasting room is filled with whimsical touches.

Wines include premium Black Swift series Cab Franc, Pinot Noir, Chard, and Riesling, plus Hatch 'Octobubble' rosé sparkling, Cab Sauv, Cab Franc, and Muscat, among others.

Same owners as Perseus in Naramata. Reservations required for groups of 6+.

*CEDARCREEK ESTATE WINERY

5445 Lakeshore Rd, Kelowna
(778)738-1027
www.cedarcreek.bc.ca
Tasting room: Daily 10-7
Restaurant: The Terrace - Daily 11-8:30
Tasting fee: $5 pp WWP
Wine Prices: $13-78

What a view! This is one of the original wineries in the province, a substantial property, popular for its award winning Riesling, Viognier, Chardonnay, Pinot Gris, Merlot, Syrah and Pinot Noir, plus Pinot rosé, and especially their premium Platinum series wines.

Whites and Pinot Noir are grown up in the cooler north, and the remaining reds plus Viognier in hot Osoyoos, like their flagship bold blend The Last Word (Cab Sauv, Merlot, Cab Franc, Malbec).

The home vineyard hosts weddings, plus yoga and painting classes, concerts, and has many private tour options including a walk through the vines with a sommelier (from $30 pp). Their well regarded restaurant, the Terrace, serves lunch and dinner, and also offers seated tastings of portfolio wines (from $25 pp).

Same ownership as Mission Hill and CheckMate.

KITSCH WINES

3330 Neid Rd, Kelowna
(778)478-4288
www.kitschwines.ca
Tasting room: Daily 12-5
Tasting fee: $3 pp WWP
Wine Prices: $20-22

Housed in a monumental stone faced estate that belongs on the cover of a shelter mag, Kitsch has a killer view over the lake, and a vibrant tasting room featuring colourful striped art and for good measure, a canoe.

Currently, their portfolio includes popular Chardonnay, Pinot Gris and Riesling. Spring 2017 releases will include Pinot Noir, several Rieslings, and a rosé.

*SANDHILL WINES (CALONA WINERY BOUTIQUE)

1125 Richter St, Kelowna
(250)762-9144
www.sandhillwines.ca

Tasting room: Daily 10-6
Tasting fee: $6 pp WWP
Wine Prices: $15-34

An urban wine tasting experience in this freshly renovated historic building in downtown Kelowna, which brings a hip historic loft to mind with its soaring ceilings and bright orange chairs.

There aren't vineyard views, but you will be treated to an interactive tasting with screens displaying each of the sites grapes are sourced from, and a goodly selection of wines to taste, often over 20, ranging from Gretzky's full bodied reds (yes, the Great One), to Calona's easy drinking wines, but the best are Sandhill's Small Lot reserve wines (Viognier, Chardonnay, Syrah, Merlot, Sangiovese, Syrah, Barbera, Malbec). You can also taste the Howard Soon label, a special winemaker project available exclusively at the winery.

Sandhill is owned by Peller Estates, whose brands include Red Rooster, Trius, and Thirty Bench, among others.

SPIERHEAD WINERY

3950 Spiers Rd, Kelowna
(250)763-7777
www.spierheadwinery.com
Tasting room: Daily 11-5:30
Restaurant: Patio Bistro - Weds-Sun 12-6, weather permitting
Tasting fee: $5 pp WWP
Wine Prices: $18-35

Cool climate premium Pinot Noir is the big draw to this bright gold winery.

Pinots are lighter bodied, on the elegant side (you might hear them called Burgundian), and include a selection of site specific bottlings from a variety of Dijon clones, along with Chard, Pinot Gris, Riesling, and Pursuit and Vanguard red Bordeaux blends.

Nibbles available on the patio include thin crust pizza from their outdoor oven, salads, olives, hummus, charcuteries, and cheeses, all favouring local, organic ingredients.

*SUMMERHILL PYRAMID WINERY

4870 Chute Lake Rd, Kelowna
(250)764-8000
www.summerhill.bc.ca
Tasting room: Daily 9-7
Restaurant: Sunset Organic Bistro - Daily 11-9
Tasting fee: Complimentary-$10 pp Premium WWP, Icewine $3 per sample WWP Icewine
Wine Prices: $20-148
Organic

A pyramid in BC? Yes, Summerhill has one, built to house their cellar. This quirky family-run winery on the shore east of Kelowna is well respected for their commitment to organic and biodynamic principles, and proudly call Summerhill 'the most visited winery in Canada'.

Best known for their traditional method sparkling wines, like the Cipes Brut and Cipes Blanc de Blanc, make sure to try their still wines too: easy drinking Alive red and white blends, plus Chardonnay, and Riesling. For reds: Pinot Noir, Sangiovese/Merlot, Merlot, Syrah, Zweigelt, and Baco Noir. If you enjoy the sweeter stuff, they make Icewine from Chard, Merlot, and Zweigelt.

Fresh wine country fare is served at the lakeview Sunset Bistro, with plenty of salads, pasta, and pizza on offer.

*TANTALUS VINEYARDS

1670 DeHart Rd, Kelowna
(250)764-0078
www.tantalus.ca
Tasting room: Daily 10-6
Tasting fee: Complimentary-$4 pp WWP, Icewine $3-5 WWP of Icewine
Wine Prices: $17-65

A mover and shaker in the Riesling world, Tantalus is one of the best regarded producers in Canada. They make excellent

Pinot Noir too, as well as Chardonnay, and a Pinot Noir/Pinot Meunier rosé, both Riesling and Pinot Noir bubblies, plus Syrah and Riesling Icewines.

The winery's tasting room is a modern delight, with a wall of glass overlooking vineyards and lake (the slopes being especially pretty in Autumn when the leaves turn gold), and a collection of beautiful carved masks which also feature on their labels. This is a special vineyard site, with some older vine plantings (1978 Riesling, 1985 Pinot Noir & Chardonnay). Honey for sale in the shop was produced by the bees housed in their vineyards.

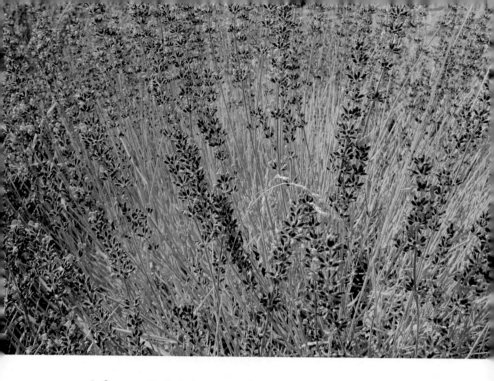

LAKE COUNTRY

A beautiful area, with plenty of room for contemplation, and slower pace than nearby Kelowna. You're never far from a water view here.

*50TH PARALLEL ESTATE

17101 Terrace View Rd, Lake Country
(250)766-3408
www.50thparallel.com
Tasting room: Daily 10:30-6
Tasting fee: $5-8 pp WWP
Wine Prices: $19-32

Ambitious and delicious. A newer winery custom built to house a gravity fed winemaking area in full view of the tasting room.

Take it all in: the live edge wood bar, polished concrete floors, and shiny fermentation tanks.

Enjoy warm hospitality at the standing bar while enjoying their signature Pinot Noir and Chardonnay, plus Pinot Gris, Gew, and Pinot Noir rosé wines made by ex-Quail's Gate winemaker Grant Stanley. The next phase of building will include a restaurant, and guest suites to take advantage of the lake view. In the meantime, nearby Sparkling Hill Resort is a fantastic spot to stay.

*ARROWLEAF CELLARS

1574 Camp Rd, Lake Country
(250)766-2992
www.arrowleafcellars.com
Tasting room: Daily 10-6
Restaurant: The Kitchen at Arrowleaf - Daily 11:30-5:30
Tasting fee: Complimentary-$5 pp WWP
Wine Prices: $14-43

Great values here at Arrowleaf, best known for their whites, including the popular off-dry Snow Tropics (Riesling/Gew). Their Riesling is a tremendous deal, and they also do Pinot Gris, Gew, Bacchus, plus Merlot, Zweigelt, Pinot Noir, and Solstice blend (Merlot, Zweigelt) for reds. Sweet options include both a late harvest and Icewine made from Vidal.

The modern and appealing winery houses a gift area, plus they have a large picnic area with incredible views, where you can enjoy wine by the glass.

Sandwiches, salads, cheese plates, and sweet treats like brownies are available from The Kitchen.

GRAY MONK ESTATE WINERY

1055 Camp Rd, Lake Country
(250)766-3168
www.graymonk.com
Tasting room: Daily 9-9
Restaurant: The Grapevine - Daily 11:30-9
Tasting fee: Complimentary-$5 pp for Reserve wines
Wine Prices: $17-39

A BC institution, the Heiss family were pioneers, starting their winery in 1972. They have some of the oldest plantings in the valley, including the first Pinot Gris in Canada which was originally sourced from Alsace. The name comes from the Austrian for Pinot Gris, *grauar mönch*, which translates to 'Gray Monk'.

There's a capacious tasting area where you can sample the wines, including their top tier Odyssey Series Cab Sauv, white Meritage, or signature rosé and white bubblies. Their Riesling and Ehrenfelser are great values.

The winery provides free 45 minute guided tours for small groups, hourly from 11-4.

Enjoy a view over the lake while you have a lunch or dinner of well prepared classic dishes, like pan seared steelhead and roast duck, at their Grapevine restaurant.

SIMILKAMEEN VALLEY

Sweeping views meet rustic paradise in this verdant river valley filled with organic vineyards and orchards, roadside fruit stands, and a relaxed country charm.

Step away from the relative hustle and bustle to explore the up and coming "sunny Similkameen", also known as the Organic Farming Capital of Canada. It's an open secret that some of the best grapes in BC are grown here. Extra hours of sunshine make it possible to ripen even big reds like Petit Verdot.

The tasting rooms are quieter and less rushed, the easygoing pace giving you a chance to soak in the valley's warm winds, birdsong, and ponder the shapes formed by cloud shadows racing over the hills.

CAWSTON

This quiet little town a few minutes south-east of Keremeos is an endearingly bucolic hidden gem. It's home to several small producers, along with one of the best regarded wineries in Canada.

The prettiest and most scenic route for the short drive between Keremeos and Cawston is Upper Bench/Barcello Road, which will give you a view of the local farms and wineries.

Following the winding river as it snakes south from Cawston along the Crowsnest Highway, you'll get a glimpse of waving hay fields, benches of vineyards, and the velvety sagebrush desert running up into the hills on the way to Osoyoos.

EAU VIVRE WINERY & VINEYARDS

716 Lowe Drive, Cawston
(250)499-2655
www.eauvivrewinery.ca
Tasting room: Daily 10:30-5:30
Tasting fee: $5 pp WWP
Wine Prices: $17-27

A little piece of the French countryside in tiny Cawston. The tasting room, and small chateau-inspired house beyond the vines, are washed in creamy yellow stucco. Delicious award-winning Pinot Noir is a particular draw, along with Gewürztraminer, Riesling, Cab Franc, and Malbec. Blends include an aromatic white called Cinq Blanc (Pinot Gris, Viognier, Sauvignon Blanc, Riesling, Gew), and their big Bordeaux style red, Buddhafull.

Eau Vivre has a welcoming and low-key tasting room, with grassy patio. Keep an eye out for packs of roving baby quail as you pull into the parking area, as they like to patrol near the large willow trees.

*FORBIDDEN FRUIT WINERY

620 Sumac Rd, Cawston
(250)499-2649
www.forbiddenfruitwines.com
Tasting room: Daily 10-6
Tasting fee: By donation
Wine Prices: $19-30
Organic

Champions of fruit wines and organic farming. The cozy tasting room has an arts and crafts vibe, and a patio to relax on. Quiet and tucked away from the hustle and bustle, the winery (which makes fruit and grape-based wines) is located on Ven'Amour Organic Farms.

Standouts include their Earth Series Cabernet Sauvignon, and Merlot, along with Pearsuasion, a dry pear-based table wine, and fortified Apricot Mistelle, a luscious apricot dessert wine (other fortifieds include cherry, apples with honey, and plum). There's also an incredibly tasty peach sparkling wine called Flirt.

The winery offers their Harvest Moon guest cabin for rent, which accommodates larger groups, and features a screened porch with views over the river, hot tub, and BBQ ($225-275/ night).

LITTLE FARM WINERY

2155 Newton Rd, Cawston
(250)317-8796
www.littlefarmwinery.ca
Tasting room: Thurs-Sun 11-5
Tasting fee: $5 pp WWP

Wine Prices: $22-26
Organic

An uber small-lot winery focused on low intervention (aka very few to zero additives) wines served in a charmingly tiny and casual winemaking shed, with a view through to their 4 acres of vineyards and the hills beyond.

The focused portfolio includes a mineral-laden dry Riesling, Pied de Cuve natural Riesling and barrel fermented textural Chardonnay, plus a savoury Cabernet Franc Rosé, and Cabernet Franc.

Run by a husband and wife team that includes one of the only Masters of Wine in Canada, Little Farm is creating some very interesting wines, with a truly Similkameen sensibility.

*OROFINO VINEYARDS

2152 Barcelo Road. Cawston
(250)499-0068
www.orofinovineyards.com
Tasting room: Daily 10-5
Tasting fee: By donation
Wine Prices: $20-45

This estate winery is one of the best regarded in the Similkameen Valley, and making waves internationally too. Step into the refreshingly cool interior of their straw bale and rosy-umber stucco tasting room, to enjoy their Pinot Noir, Merlot, Syrah, Cabernet

Sauvignon, and popular Moscato bubbly, which all show off the pure fruit flavours this valley is known for. Their Rieslings are particularly sought after, intense and vibrant (a standout is their Old Vines Riesling). They also produce tasty Chardonnay, Pinot Gris, and Gamay.

Check their website for occasional dinner events held in their garden courtyard with clay pizza oven, or stay in one of their two new guest suites on the property, the nicest accommodation in the valley ($199-259/night).

*TWISTED HILLS CRAFT CIDER

2080 Ritchie Dr, Cawston
(250)488-4256
www.twistedhills.ca
Tasting room: Daily 11-5:30
Tasting fee: Complimentary
Wine Prices: $7-18
Organic

Twisted Hills has the distinction of being the only cidery included in this guide. If you're winetripping through the Similkameen, it shouldn't be missed. Master cidermaker Kaylan is crafting her artisan bubbly with organically grown historic dessert and cider apples (like Orange Pippins) from their own estate, using Champagne yeasts. The crisp Pippin's Fate, and off-dry Kingston's Twist are excellent. The Sparkling Orchard has a touch of pear for sweetness.

A refreshing stop on a hot day, with a rustic tasting room-garage open to the surrounding orchards. Can sell out in August, so check website.

KEREMEOS

One of the most notable sights of the region is the row of fruit stands and their vivid painted signs as you approach the historic farming town of Keremeos. Beckoning from the stands are peaches, apricots, cherries, melons, tomatoes, herbs, garlic, walnuts, and more, all produced from the "fruit basket of Canada". Autumn is a wonder of pumpkins, stacked into elaborate displays.

Long sunny days combined with cool nights, and refreshing breezes keep the fruit healthy while it gets nicely ripened, resulting in pure, rounded, and juicy flavours.

Head over the Keremeos Bypass Road to connect to Penticton and the Okanagan Valley, or continue south along the Crowsnest to explore this beautiful river valley on your way to Cawston and Osoyoos.

*CLOS DU SOLEIL WINERY

2568 Upper Bench Rd, Keremeos
(250)499-2381
www.closdusoleil.ca
Tasting room: Daily 10-5
Tasting fee: Complimentary
Wine Prices: $20-60

A very well regarded premium producer, with the most elegant tasting room in the Similkameen. Recently opened, the teal blue entry and white awnings evoke a Parisian storefront, while the classic metal siding reminds you that you're in a farming community. The winery's name, meaning an enclosure of sun, comes from the heat trap formed by the mountains behind the vineyard.

The bright and polished tasting area offers a selection of Bordeaux-inspired wines including a zesty standout Sauvignon Blanc/Semillon blend called Capella, and their oaked version Fumé Blanc. They also do a fruity Pinot Blanc. Richly ripe yet balanced reds are putting this area on the map, such as their Cab/Merlot, and Célestiale (Cab Sauv, Merlot, Cab Franc, Petit Verdot, and Malbec) blends. PS: don't miss the vibrant and sweet Saturn, made from late harvested Sauv Blanc.

CORCELETTES ESTATE WINERY

2582 Upper Bench Rd, Keremeos
(250)499-5595
www.corcelletteswine.ca
Tasting room: Daily 10:30-5:30
Tasting fee: $5 pp WWP
Wine Prices: $18-100

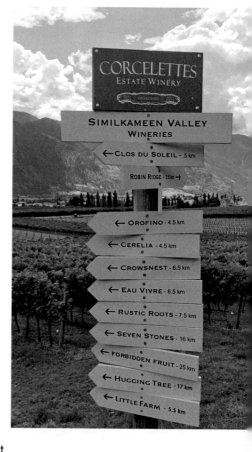

An up and coming small-lot family winery, whose tasting room offers expansive views over the upper Similkameen Valley. A tasting here is a pleasure, as you'll likely have the chance to speak with winemaker Charlie.

Crafted with passion are reds Pinot Noir, Merlot, Syrah, and a peppery Zweigelt rosé. For whites: smooth Chasselas, Gewürztraminer, and blend Trivium (Chasselas, Gew, Pinot Gris). Their flagship wine is called Menhir, a bold Cab Sauv/Syrah, named for the ancient standing stone on their family farm in Switzerland. Creamy bubbly Santé is made from Viognier, Chardonnay, and Pinot Gris.

ROBIN RIDGE WINERY

2686 Middle Bench Rd, Keremeos
(250)499-5504
www.robinridgewinery.com
Tasting room: Daily 10-5:30
Tasting fee: $3 pp WWP
Wine Prices: $16-30

A country charmer of a winery, named for the plump robins you'll spot perching nearby, making some very tasty wines at fair prices. The spicy, full flavoured Gewürztraminer is a winner. They've also got a gently oaked and mineral laden Chardonnay, and sweeter late harvested Chard. Cabernet Franc is a particular standout, a steal for the quality level, ripe and smooth on the palate. Other reds include Pinot Noir, Merlot, and Big Bird blend (Merlot, Cab Sauv, Cab Franc, Petit Verdot).

One of the only wineries in the valley doing a double curtain style of vine growing, be sure to check these interestingly shaped vines out on the way in to the casual and very hospitable tasting room.

GETTING AROUND SAFELY

Did you know BC has extremely strict drinking and driving laws? If you're from BC, you'll definitely know we're subject to hefty fines for any phone use while driving!

The roads in the Okanagan and Similkameen have many twists and turns, including busy country highways with no medians. These are just a few reasons why when you're winetripping, you need to have a designated driver who won't be drinking. Never drink and drive.

All winery tasting rooms will happily provide you with a spittoon, but beware that even with spitting out wine you will still absorb alcohol into your system.

Tour Guides

One of the best ways to get around is with a dedicated tour company. A bonus of using a private tour guide, is that the best have built relationships with the local wineries that will help you get the most out of your visit. Here are some of the top wine touring companies that offer guided private tours:

Experience Wine Tours

www.experiencewinetours.ca

TF (866)826-8687

This company is dialled in to the very best wineries; I've seen their air-conditioned vans at a selection of thoughtfully chosen producers. They also arrange delicious picnic lunches for their guests. $125-165 pp.

Wicked Wine

www.wickedwinetours.com

(250)864-9453

Every time I see a group touring with this company, they're having fun. They've designed tours for each of the Okanagan's sub-regions, and you can choose to include lunch or have them book a restaurant reservation for you. $60-150 pp.

Nixdorf Classic Cars

www.nixdorfclassiccars.com

(250)494-4111

Have you ever wanted to be chauffeured around wine country in a convertible 1963 Cadillac? How about a teal 1960 Oldsmobile? Well, this is the place to call. Up to four guests can ride in style, enjoying the view from a beautiful restored convertible. They'll arrange a picnic lunch for you to enjoy upon request, and can help you choose the wineries or take you where you want to go. Car buffs would enjoy a stroll through their Summerland showroom too. From $120/hr, minimum 2 hours.

Wine Shuttles

Before you book, ask at your hotel or restaurant if they provide a dedicated shuttle, several offer an evening service in high season to get you to and from popular restaurants and wineries.

OK Wine Shuttle

www.okwineshuttle.ca

(250)495-3278

A hop-on hop-off touring company in the south Okanagan from Penticton to Osoyoos, running from 11am - 5pm for $65 pp, that stops at major hotels and a wide selection of wineries. They also offer cost-effective private tours that seat up to 14 guests from $75 pp.

Coconut Express

www.thecoconutexpress.com
(250)462-9396

Offers special event shuttles between concerts, dinners, restaurants, and hotels from $20 pp. You can also book to join other small groups of 2-5 people on tours of Naramata and Summerland, from $50 pp. They offer private group tours departing Penticton or Osoyoos from $297.

Getting to the Okanagan

By Car

By car from Vancouver, getting to the Okanagan takes about four hours. From Vancouver, take the Trans-Canada Highway #1 to Hope. At Hope, you'll have the choice of taking two routes:

The #5 Coquilhalla route is the most efficient way to reach Kelowna in the northern Okanagan Valley. It used to be a toll road, so is generally in good condition. Please note that there are often police speed traps along this road, with corresponding fines.

The more scenic option is Highway #3, called the Crowsnest (look for the white road signs featuring a black crow symbol). Improvements over the past few years have greatly enhanced this country highway, although there are still a couple of spots which have active work being completed. This route will take you through Manning Park, where you can grab a coffee, stretch your legs, and admire the ground squirrels and swallows at the lodge. The route then swoops into the Similkameen Valley where the road rises above the winding Similkameen River. At Keremeos, you'll have the option of heading east using the 3A Bypass connector to Penticton, or continuing south on Highway 3 through the charming fruit stands of Cawston before heading over the desert hills to Osoyoos.

From Oct-Mar, all roads require snow tires and for you to carry tire chains in your car.

By Air

Penticton has a regional airport with direct flights connecting between Vancouver and Calgary, provided by Air Canada and WestJet. A flight from Vancouver is about one hour, and from Calgary about 80 minutes.

Kelowna has an international airport with direct flights connecting between Vancouver (1 hour), Calgary (1 hour), Toronto (4 hours 40 minutes), and Seattle (1 hour), among others.

Both airports are serviced by major car rental companies, with reservations highly recommended.

You can take an airport shuttle: The Coconut Express (www.thecoconutexpress.com) has stops between Penticton and the Kelowna airport, plus a Penticton hotel to Penticton airport route. Let's Go Transportation (www.letsgotransportation.ca) serves both airports with stops through the whole Okanagan between Osoyoos and Kelowna.

WINE COUNTRY YEAR

Unofficially, the winetripping season opens as of the May long weekend. Some of the best times for touring are just ahead of this in early May, before the crowds arrive. Early October is another great time to visit, as you'll see the vines turn vibrant golds and reds, and avoid the busier July-September months. Although a chill can descend, you'll get more space to rest your elbows at the tasting bars.

The busiest times are of course Summer weekends of July, August and early September, although you'll find even weekdays can be buzzing. If you're travelling during these months, your best bet is to minimize Friday-Sunday touring, or head out as an early bird to tour in the morning.

In high season, reservations for meals, tastings, and accommodations become imperative to achieve a disappointment-free trip, doubly so if you are travelling as part of a group (for groups, pre-booking during high season is a must)!

Keep in mind the times listed in this guide are based on high season hours, and are also subject to change.

Winter in the valleys is peaceful but can be a bit sleepy. Many of the smaller wineries close their tasting rooms (except for private appointments) during October, re-opening briefly for winter open house events. The larger wineries and urban wineries are most likely to operate year round.

Spring

The vineyards spring to life around April, when the vines shift from sleepy rows of empty canes, and experience bud burst and their new leaves leaves unfurl. Tasting rooms also spring to life in April.

Summer

Summers in the Okanagan and Similkameen can get super hot, over 35 degrees Celsius on a good day. Make sure you've got a sun hat, sunscreen, and if possible a cooler to protect any wine you'll be transporting from being cooked. You can always cool off by hitting the pool or lake for a swim.

One of the key factors in the area that helps keep the local wines' flavours vibrant, is that even on hot sunny days, the temperature can drop quickly in the evening. Some people say it's like putting the grapes in the refrigerator at night to stay fresh. The technical term for this temperature swing is 'diurnal shift'. Practically, it means that you should be sure to take along a sweater or light coat for the evenings, even in summertime.

Keep in mind it's a big valley, and Osoyoos in the south can be much warmer than Kelowna and Lake Country to the north. Harvest can begin in August, and go well into Autumn.

Autumn

If you're lucky enough to witness the turning colours of the Autumn vines, it's something you won't soon forget. Leaves transform from green to intense burgundy, gold and amber as the season shifts. This is also the season for magically sweet Icewine, which is usually harvested starting in November depending on weather, and continuing into Winter.

Winter

It gets chilly in winter here, but perhaps not as cold as you might expect (vines start dying off if a sustained freeze of -10C happens). Head for the local ski hills to catch some fine BC powder, or put on a toque and mitts as you explore the area. The largest wineries stay open most of the year, but if you want to go winetripping, call ahead to confirm and book appointments.

VINTAGE GUIDE

During your touring, you'll likely see youthful whites and rosés (released between 1-2 years old), and reds from 2-5 years old for release. When the wines are ready to drink depends on your personal taste, and the particular vintage, but you'll soon pick up whether you like your reds with just a couple of years of age when they're young, firm, and fruity, or with an extra few years to round things out.

2016: On track to be another sterling vintage (fingers crossed)! There's been more rain than usual during June and July, but that's OK as there's been plenty of sun during August and September, putting the season just a few weeks ahead of schedule.

2015: A hot, dry vintage with potential for excellence and intensity. A forest fire threatened the Golden Mile Bench, but luckily the wineries there were spared. Whites in general are fuller bodied than usual, with extra ripeness resulting in higher potential alcohol levels. Reds benefitted from plenty of sunshine, and a long warm Autumn. Word on the street is 'vintage of the century'.

2014: Hot, hot, hot. Another banner year, with warm temperatures bringing substantial concentration and ripe tannins in reds, and high quality fruity whites, that managed to retain freshness with solid acidity levels. A key vintage for reds.

2013: A rainy Autumn means wine quality will vary depending on when the winemaker harvested - before the rains or after. Overall it was a warm growing season with record crops, setting the stage for good potential from quality minded producers. Excellent Icewine resulted from a January freeze.

2012: An excellent vintage with consistently high quality. A banner year for red wines in particular, which are drinking very well now.

2011: Chillier than usual, expect lighter wines with slightly lower than average alcohol levels. A challenging year for some producers, who had to work hard in the vineyards to ensure even ripening, but were paid off with very good quality fruit.

2010: A rainier than normal, and cooler growing season followed by blessedly good Autumn weather, means you can expect higher acidity wines with staying power. A desirably chilly November made it a great year for Icewine.

WINE VISITOR CENTRES & REGIONAL ASSOCIATIONS

Each sub-region hosts a visitor centre with plenty of helpful information, touring maps, and more. These make a good stop if you want to find additional information about local wineries, accommodation, wine tours, restaurants and activities. Associations for each sub-region represent member wineries, and provide helpful maps and guides.

Kelowna

544 Harvey Avenue
(250)861-1515
www.tourismkelowna.com

Kelowna - West

2376 Dobbin Rd
(250)768-2712
www.visitwestside.com

Okanagan Falls

#2 - 5350 9th Ave
(250)497-6260
www.okfalls.ca/visit_okfalls

Oliver

6431 Station St
(778)439-2363
www.winecapitalofcanada.com

Osoyoos

#236 - 15 Park Place
(778)699-2044
www.destinationosoyoos.com

Peachland

5684 Beach Ave
(250)767-2455
www.destinationpeachland.com

Penticton

553 Vees Dr
(250)276-2170
www.visitpenticton.com

Summerland

15600 Hwy 97
(250)494-2686
www.tourismsummerland.com

Similkameen

417 – 7th Avenue, Keremeos
(250)499-5225
www.similkameenvalley.com

Regional Winery Associations

Oliver Osoyoos Wine Country
www.oliverosoyoos.com

Okanagan Falls Winery Association
www.ofwa.ca

Naramata Bench Wineries Association
www.naramatabench.com

Summerland's Bottleneck Drive Winery Association
www.bottleneckdrive.com

West Kelowna's Westside Wine Trail
www.thewestsidewinetrail.com

Kelowna Fab 5 Wineries
www.kelownafabfive.ca

Lake Country's The Scenic Sip
www.scenicsip.ca

Similkameen Wineries Association
www.similkameenwine.com

FUN ACTIVITIES

If you want to spread your wings, here are some unique activities the valleys have to offer. They may just add a certain je ne sais quois to your adventure.

Canadian Jetpack Adventures

Have you ever wanted to strap on wake boots and lake fly?
Multiple locations
1.855.359.2232
www.canadianjetpackadventures.com

Osoyoos Desert Model Railroad

Model train fans will love the miniature cities set up here.
11611 115th St, Osoyoos
(250)495-6842
www.osoyoosrailroad.com

Kettle Valley Steam Railway

Pretend you're on Platform 9&3/4 at this beautiful historic passenger train.
18404 Bathville Rd, Summerland
(250)494-8422
www.kettlevalleyrail.org

Okanagan Observatory

The Okanagan is a superlative star gazing area, and the public can enjoy the constellations from a special viewing spot.

4 kms up Big White Rd from Hwy 33, Kelowna

(250)300-8759

www.okanaganobservatory.ca

Penticton Farmer's Market

One of the best markets anywhere; has it all, from baked goods to fresh veg, and even wine. Saturdays Apr 23-Oct 29, 8:30-1.

100 block of Main St

www.pentictonfarmersmarket.org

Heatstroke Cycle Electric Bikes

Take a biking wine tour, with help from the bike's motor to get up those Golden Mile hills.

#225 - 15 Park Place (Watermark Resort)

(778)437-2453

www.heatstrokecycle.com

Desert Centre

Explore Canada's only semi-arid desert on a boardwalk guided tour, and learn more about the unique flora and fauna.

14580 146th Ave, Osoyoos

(250)495-2470

www.desert.org

Predator Ridge Golf & Sparkling Hill Resort

If you're mad about golf, this is a quality course. For spa lovers, visit heaven at nearby Sparkling Hill Resort.

Predator Ridge - 301 Village Centre Pl, Vernon

www.predatorridge.com/golf

Sparkling Hill - 888 Sparkling Pl, Vernon
www.sparklinghill.com

Similkameen Fruit Stands

Save room in your trunk for the incredible selection of farm fresh fruits and veg at these seasonal roadside stands.
Along the Crowsnest Hwy in Keremeos & Cawston

Okanagan Lavender Herb Farm

Lavender galore, visit in July to enjoy peak bloom. Tours $15 pp.
4380 Takla Rd, Kelowna
(250)764-7795
www.okanaganlavender.com

Penticton River Channel

A popular way to spend a sunny day, bring a tube or rent, to float down the channel, with a shuttle to take you back to your car. The launch site is on Riverside Dr.

Planet Bee Honey Farm & Meadery

Fans of the sweet nectar will love watching the bees here.
5011 Bella Vista Rd, Vernon
(250)452-8088
www.planetbee.com

Hike Peach Cliff Lookout

Enjoy the staggering views from this lookout spot in Okanagan Falls. Instructions for accessing the hike off McLean Creek Rd are on the website.
www.exploreoliverbc.com/blog/hike-peach-cliff-okanagan-falls

WINE TIPS & TASTING ROOM ETIQUETTE

Wine Clubs

Most of the wineries in this guide offer special benefits to wine club members, ranging from discounts on wine, exclusive or complimentary tasting experiences, or access to vacation rentals among their vineyards.

Another popular benefit is being first in line for purchasing special edition or small lot wines that aren't available in stores. If you fall in love with a particular producer, it's worthwhile to sign up for their wine club for some serious perks. Most clubs are free to join, although there is generally a minimum annual purchase for members.

Booking Private Tastings

Winery websites, which you'll see listed throughout this guide, are the best spot to get the 411 on special events, tastings, and tours, or to book a tasting appointment. Most wineries prefer groups of six or more call in advance to book a time at the tasting bar.

You can also check out www.vinovisit.com as several wineries list private events and tastings that can be booked on this portal.

Tasting Room Tips

The tasting rooms featured in this guide range from rustic warehouse settings, to state of the art multi-million dollar temples to wine. There are a few tips that will help you feel comfortable no matter what kind of winery you're visiting:

Avoid perfumes & scents: They greatly reduce your, and that of the people around you, ability to smell and taste the wines.

Make friends: You never know who you're talking to, the person at the counter could be the winemaker or owner. Whoever it is, working in a busy tasting room can be hard work, so don't forget the pleasantries.

Feel free to spit out wine or empty your glass into the spittoons: Spitting out or pouring out your wine won't hurt anyone's feelings (whether because you don't want to imbibe, you can't finish your sample, or you didn't like it). In fact, you might get even more respect! If no bucket is in sight, just ask, there's one tucked away that can be brought out for you.

Establish codewords: I've got a friend that has a couple of codewords to tell her husband whether she liked a wine or not. I highly recommend you do likewise with your fellow winetrippers, so you can subtly tell each other what you're thinking in not so many words.

Be respectful of other visitors: Try to be space aware if there's a squeeze at the bar, offering room for others to be welcomed. Make conversation with other visitors and your host, this can be the best place to get insider intel on recently visited wineries and restaurants.

Let management know: Everyone wants to have a great time, but sometimes the stars just don't align that way. Do let management know if something went sideways, it's only fair to give them a chance to make things right.

Practice moderation: Hey, we all like to have fun and drink wine, but pace yourself! Make sure you drink lots of water while tasting to stay hydrated.

Buy some wine if you liked it: There's no rule that you have to buy wine at every winery you visit, especially if it wasn't to your taste, or you didn't enjoy the experience (hopefully that doesn't happen).

It's a nice courtesy to buy a bottle or two of your favourite wine, and often you'll find wineries will credit your tasting fee against your purchase. If you've booked a private appointment, it's generally understood that you're there to taste and buy.

Ask for a box or bring a cooler in your trunk: Most wineries provide 12-bottle boxes free of charge. Savvy winetrippers will have a cooler so their precious bottles won't get sun scorched in the trunk.

Don't try to do too much: 3-6 wineries in a day will be plenty.

Dress for success: While the tasting rooms are fairly casual, I've noticed service is always best when guests have made an effort to dress nicely.

Wine Tasting Technique

Here are the four easy steps to follow to feel like a pro when tasting wine:

Step 1: See - Tilt your glass or hold it up to the light to admire and assess the colour and clarity.

Step 2: Swirl & Smell - When you swirl your glass, you're oxygenating the wine, and creating a 'wine vortex' which will enhance the aromas. Hold your glass at the bottom of the stem to get maximum swirl action.

Step 3: Sip - Yes, finally, the good stuff! How many flavors can you taste, and are they different from what others are picking up?

Step 4: Savour - How long do the pleasant flavours linger on your palate? A long and complex finish is a sign of a high quality wine.

These steps start to come naturally. Soon, you'll have an idea what to expect from certain grapes, and even vintages and sub-regions of the valley!

Pairing Food & Wine

You've probably heard lots of different rules for pairing wine with your meal; these are some general guidelines to keep in mind. Keep experimenting and don't be afraid to break the rules.

Intensity & body = Match intensity with intensity, and body with body. If you're having a big, bold meal, choose a big, bold wine. If you're dining on something delicate and ethereal, choose a delicate and light wine.

Spicy foods = Pair well with slightly sweet, or ripe wines with soft tannins. Spicy heat can limit your ability to taste sugar, so having a chili-spiked dish with a dry wine will make the wine taste extra dry and even astringent.

Rich or acidic dishes = Creamy pasta, fried foods, and acidic foods like tomato or citrus, all pair well with a higher acidity wine. The acidity in the wine helps to balance out that in the food, and can enliven heavier dishes.

Salty foods = Can make tannic or high alcohol wines taste bitter or boozy. Choose a wine with sweetness, a ripe profile, or juicy acidity instead.

Red wine & fish = Avoid pairing tannic red wines with fish. They can interact to create a strange metallic taste. Ignore people who say you can't have red wine with fish though, lighter varieties such as Pinot Noir or Gamay paired with seafood can be delightful.

Sweet wines = When pairing a dessert, try to choose a wine that is sweeter than the dish. The sugar in desserts can mask the sweetness of a wine, making it taste flat. Sweet wines can also shine with salty foods like cheese or olives.

Think sparkling = It's way easier to pair a wine to a meal, than to create a meal to match a specific wine. The exception is bubbly, which goes with everything.

GRAPE GUIDE

The Okanagan and Similkameen are starting to build some major street cred in the world of wine. Quality is high and continues to make gains every year. In particular, pay attention to these grape varietals which are becoming BC stars: Syrah, Cabernet Franc, Pinot Noir, Chardonnay, Gewürztraminer, and Riesling. Keep track of which grapes you've tried in the Notes section at the back of this guide!

If you're curious about what's growing in those gorgeous vineyards, here's a primer on some of the most planted red and white grapes in British Columbia, and what you can expect in your glass:

Reds:

Cabernet Franc: dark fruit, black pepper, cable of finesse, and can have a slight herbaceous note.

Cabernet Sauvignon: bold and structured, with black fruit, mint, violets, and graphite.

Gamay Noir: a lighter, fruity red, with lower tannins.

Malbec: makes deep and dark reds, with plum and black fruit notes.

Marechal Foch: a hybrid grape capable of making inky dark wines with mocha and blackberry flavours.

Merlot: plush and plummy, with easygoing tannins, often used as a blending partner to balance more structured grapes.

Petit Verdot: structured tannins, with graphite, purple flower, and bold black cherry and blueberry notes.

Pinot Noir: red berries, sweet earth, this can make a lighter, delicate, elegant red wine.

Syrah/Shiraz: same grape, different styles, with black fruit, can have smokey and peppery highlights. Shiraz is the fruitier version, Syrah is more savoury.

Zweigelt: an Austrian grape with lively spiciness, and red and black fruit notes.

Whites:

Chardonnay: a chameleon, ranging from bright, light apples and lemon in stainless steel, to creamy, tropical, and even toasty vanilla if oaked. "ABC" is slang for *anything but Chardonnay*, hopefully if you feel this way, you'll give it another chance.

Chenin Blanc: vibrant acidity meets apple and pear, and sometimes a waxy or lanolin note.

Ehrenfelser: a descendent of Riesling, with good tolerance to the cold, and tropical fruit notes.

Gewürztraminer: the "spice grape", floral, with roses, lychee, orange blossom, and good weight.

Ortega: a cold resistant grape often used in making sweet wines, with floral and stone fruit flavours.

Pinot Blanc: fruity ranging to tropical notes, round bodied, and also enjoyable as a sweet wine.

Pinot Gris/Pinot Grigio: same grape, different styles, with citrus and peach flavours. Pinot Gris is riper and fruitier, Pinot Grigio, lighter, more acidic and citric.

Riesling: can range from dry, steely lime and mineral, to peach, honey, even diesel, and has a characteristic bright acidity. Makes excellent sweet wines.

Sauvignon Blanc: melon, gooseberry, and grassy notes, plus citrus and guava, with zesty refreshing acidity.

Viognier: a fuller bodied white, with peach and floral notes, and notable silky texture.

WINE WORDS GLOSSARY

Acidity: Responsible for the juicy, mouthwatering, zingy, and vibrant feelings in your mouth. Acidity is a very good thing for wine to have; without, it can be soft, flabby or forgettable. Having good levels of acid is also a key factor in pairing with food. Grapes that can potentially have higher levels are Pinot Grigio, Riesling, Sauvignon Blanc, Chenin, Cabernet Sauvignon, and Sangiovese. Some folks prefer lower acid wines, and they should keep an eye out for wines from hotter sub-regions or grapes that typically show lower acidity (Merlot, oaked Chard, Gew, Pinot Gris, Viognier).

Bench: Not a place to sit after a long day, but a sloped shoulder of land. Benches you'll hear of include Black Sage Bench and the Golden Mile Bench near Oliver, and the Skaha and Naramata Benches. These make excellent vineyard sites because the sloped land gives grapes maximum sun exposure in Spring and Summer while also encouraging heavier cold air to drift downwards and away from the vines in Autumn and Winter, avoiding the dreaded vine killer known as a "frost pocket".

Clone: When we hear "Pinot Noir", it's tempting to think of just one grape, but there are many expressions or "clones" of each variety that have been bred over time, in the same way there are many shapes, sizes and scents of red roses. Some clones are chosen because they produce a particularly desirable flavour or texture, or have better pest resistance. You might see the clone mentioned on the winery's tasting sheets, and if you're interested in learning more, just ask.

Concrete eggs: Sculptural, rounded and expensive concrete fermentation vessels that are becoming more popular every year. If you do a cellar tour you might spot these near the stainless fermentation tanks. The egg shape is designed to increase circulation of the wine during fermentation, and the material imparts a silky texture.

Crush pad: This is the place where grapes come in from the fields and prepare to undergo fermentation. First, they'll be sorted, possibly de-stemmed, then crushed or pressed. "Custom crush" is slang for a facility that lets virtual winemakers (those without a winery) use the space to make their own wines.

Dry/Off-dry: When a wine tastes dry, it means there's no detectable sweetness on your palate (see Residual Sugar below). Astringent tannins can assist in making a wine taste dry. Off-dry: when the wine you're tasting's not dry, and it's not full on sweet. There's a noticeable hint of sugar.

Estate: If you hear a brand calling themselves an "estate winery", it means their grapes come from their own property and have not been bought in from other growers. Similarly, "estate bottled" denotes the wine was bottled at their winery, and not shipped elsewhere for this process.

Fermentation: The process whereby yeasts consume grape sugars and produce alcohol (plus heat and carbon dioxide). Crushed grapes and their juice are called "must" before becoming wine. White wines are usually fermented without their skins to keep aromatics fresh, and red wines are fermented with their skins to add colour and tannins. Orange wines are white wines that have had lots of "skin contact" before ferment, or can even be fermented like a red wine with skins, creating interesting flavours.

Fortified: An off-dry to sweet wine that has had a spirit such as brandy added to it. A famous example of fortified wine is Port, and you'll see many Port-inspired wines on your tasting room visits. Some, like Maverick's fortified Syrah called Fia, use brandy distilled locally.

Fruity: Used when you can taste specific fruits in the wine (such as apple, mango, cherry, plum, currant, bramble). Don't confuse fruity with sweet - a wine can be totally dry and still be really fruit forward. Grapes that are often described as fruity include Gewürztraminer, Gamay, Pinot Gris, Muscat, and Shiraz.

Full bodied: Think of body as how heavy the wine feels in your mouth as it moves over your tongue. The best way to describe a wine as light, medium or full bodied is to think of their equivalents as non-fat milk, homogenized milk, and heavy cream. Body can be a characteristic of certain types of grapes, but is also linked to how cool or hot the growing region was, and winemaking techniques. Cool area wines are often lighter bodied than the same grape grown in a toastier place. Higher levels of sugar and alcohol can make a wine feel denser too. Fuller bodied grapes include Viognier, Semillon, Zinfandel, and Shiraz.

Harvest: After grapes have undergone *veraison* (skins change colour and sugars start to develop) in mid-summer, they continue their journey to phenological ripeness. Say what? That's where a balance of sugars, acidity, and tannins in the pulp, stem, and seeds is achieved, and the harvest can begin. Choosing harvest time is somewhere between a science and an art, but other factors like weather are important too. Expect harvest to begin for white grapes in August, and for reds to continue through October depending on the vintage.

Inflorescence: This is where the vine flowers set into fruit and begin to grow into what will become a bunch. An inflorescence appears in Spring, and looks like a tiny spread out bunch of miniature green grapes.

Meritage/Bordeaux blend: Can be a red or white, inspired by the great wines of Bordeaux, France. For reds, the traditional grapes are Cab Sauv, Merlot, Cab Franc, Malbec, and Petit Verdot. For whites, Semillon and Sauv Blanc. PS: Meritage is pronounced like "heritage".

Minerality: When you taste flavours like limestone, hot rocks, petrichor (the smell after a summer rain), or slate, in your wine. A desirable thing to have.

Oak: When you hear "new oak", it means the barrel the wine was aged in was a first or second year barrel, and is imparting oaky flavours into the wine, like toast, vanilla, or caramel. After the first couple of fills, the barrels don't impart so much flavour, but play an important role in helping soften the wine with age. You might also have heard of barrel fermentation, particularly for Chardonnay, and the tasting notes often note whether the barrels were new or old. The two main types of oak used to make barrels are French and American. French has a tighter grain, giving spice and fine tannins, and American gives bolder coconut and even dill notes.

Old Vines: There's no rule how many years a vine has to be in order to be called "old". Most of BC's vineyards are less than 25 years old, so if you see Old Vines noted on a label (such as on Road 13's Chenin, or Quail's Gate Marechal Foch) it means they're old for our area. As vines age, they're said to create wines of increasing intensity and flavour, because they produce lower yields of fruit.

Pruning: The style of pruning a vine gets helps determine many things including whether it needs to be hand picked, or machine harvested, how much fruit can be cropped, and the amount of leaf cover. A commonly used style is wire trained Double Guyot where the vine has two arms with grapes hanging along the lower wires. Eagle eyed winetrippers will also spot some "double curtain" vines, a much more labour intensive and sculptural style (which can be seen at Noble Ridge, Nichol, or Robin Ridge among others), or even "bush" vines which grow like small trees with no wires.

Residual sugar (often abbreviated as 'RS'): When you drink a wine and detect sweetness, that's grape sugar that remains from after fermentation. This can happen when there's a very hot year, or the wine is designed to be off-dry (such as in a late harvest wine, where the grapes spend extra time on the vines, or unctuous super sweet Icewine, where grapes are harvested between November and January after a hard freeze - both methods concentrate sugars and flavours in a wine). If a wine has very high acidity, such as is common with Riesling, it can offset the RS on your palate and taste dry.

Rootstock: Many vines you'll see are planted on their "own roots", meaning they're not grafted. Some wineries prefer to use grafted vines, where the grape producing varietal is attached to another type of vine which forms the roots. Benefits of grafting include more control of how vigorous the vine will be, and the ability to fight Phylloxera (an aphid-like pest).

Single vineyard: A wine labelled as a Single Vineyard is site specific. It's made from a special plot of land within a vineyard that's been shown to add a particular je-ne-sais-quois to a wine.

Smoke taint: As if a vigneron didn't have enough to worry about! Smoke flavours from a nearby forest fire can be picked up by the grapes and then contaminate a wine. Not a good thing.

The Okanagan does face forest fires, such as the one that threatened several wineries in 2015. Luckily, the wines from that vintage have thus far not shown taint.

Soil: A key element in a wine's *terroir* (that special mixture of site, weather, and human care that result in a unique wine that speaks of a particular place. Soils range hugely in the valleys, as between volcanoes, glaciers, rivers and lakes, they've been mixed around. You might hear about sand on the Black Sage Bench, limestone in the Similkameen, or glacial tilth along Naramata, but every site will have a variety.

Stainless steel: If you see "stainless steel" on a label, it generally refers to the fact little or no oak was used in the wine's production. These wines usually have brighter, crisper acidity, lighter body, and don't have the oaky vanilla flavours associated with new barrels.

Tannins: That sandy, grippy, toothpaste texture you get in your mouth, especially when drinking red wine (not many whites have noticeable tannins). They come from the grape's skins, seeds, and sometimes the stalks, and are also infused into the wine as it ages in newer oak barrels. Some of the myriad ways you can describe the tannins you're tasting are: velvety, smooth, silky, light, fine-grained, chalky, gritty, powerful, or even chewy. Grapes that can have higher tannins are Cabernet Sauvignon, Nebbiolo, Petit Verdot, and Syrah.

Traditional method sparkling wine: Also known as the Champagne-method, whereby bubbles are created within the bottle via a second fermentation. This is the most time consuming and pricy method of creating bubbly.

Vertical tasting: A wine tasting of a particular wine from different vintages, side by side. Gives you a chance to learn about how the wine ages, and detect the how the character of each vintage is expressed in your glass. For example, Black Hills has vertical tastings of their Nota Bene.

Vintage: The year the grapes were grown to create a wine. If no vintage is stated, the wine is a blend from different years (such as in a non-vintage sparkling wine).

VQA: Shorthand for Vitners Quality Alliance. BC VQA certified wines must meet special standards as set by Wines of BC, and be made from 100% BC grapes. If a region is named, at least 95% of the grapes must come from that place, and if a vintage or varietal is listed then the contents must be at least 85% of what's stated.

HIDDEN TREASURES

Not all wineries have a tasting room. They might be so exclusive that they don't accept visitors. Some wine producers don't even have a winery, they use shared crush pads, or make their wines at a friendly facility, often in tiny and highly sought after quantities.

While you might not see these labels at a tasting room, you'll likely come across their names on a wine list or in a wine shop. Here are some to keep an eye out for:

Anarchist Vineyard: Their Wildfire Pinot Noir is worth seeking out.

Black Cloud: Talented Pinot Noir specialist.

Black Market Wine Co: Focused portfolio garagistes.

Bonamici: From winemaker Philip Soo, try the Merlot/Cab Franc.

CheckMate Artisanal Winery: Ultra premium small-lot Chardonnay.

Nagging Doubt: Hand crafted Chardonnay, Viognier, and Pinot Noir.

Roche: From a husband and wife team that includes Intersection's winemaker, excellent and silky wines.

Seven Directions: The best rosé in the valley, with single vineyard examples.

Vanessa Vineyard: Big reds from a fantastic Similkameen site.

BEST KNOWN FOR

I've organized these lists for winetrippers who want to plan their own custom itinerary. These are a handy tool you can use to build your own trip by referencing the longer write-ups in each region's section. The wineries below excel in their given categories.

Red Wines
Black Hills
Burrowing Owl
Clos du Soleil
Deep Roots
Fairview Cellars
Laughing Stock
Moon Curser
Painted Rock
Road 13
Van Westen

White Wines
Arrowleaf
Gehringer
Gray Monk
JoieFarm
Liquidity
Quail's Gate
Summergate
Terravista

Wild Goose

Sparkling Wine
Bella
Blue Mountain
Covert Farms
Okanagan Crush Pad
Steller's Jay (at Sumac Ridge)
Summerhill

Pinot Noir
50th Parallel
Blue Mountain
CedarCreek
Meyer
Quail's Gate
Spierhead

Riesling
Culmina
CedarCreek
Orofino
Synchromesh
Tantalus
Wild Goose

Value for Price
Arrowleaf
Gehringer Brothers
Gold Hill
Montakarn
Wild Goose

ITINERARIES

Here are some sample itineraries including standout wineries and restaurants for each sub-region in the book, to help you start planning your trip.

Similkameen: get away from the hustle and bustle to enjoy this valley's rustic charm and organic farms
Wineries: Forbidden Fruit - Little Farm Winery - Twisted Hills Craft Cider - Orofino - Robin Ridge - Clos du Soleil
Lunch: The Grist Mill, a charming historic mill with gardens
2691 Upper Bench Rd, Keremeos
www.oldgristmill.ca (250)499-2888
Dinner: Authentic Indian cuisine at Samosa Gardens (to the side of Sanderson's Fruit Stand)
3059 BC-3, Keremeos (250)499-2700

Osoyoos: enjoy those desert heat wines, ripe and delicious
Wineries: Lariana Cellars - NK'MIP - Adega on 45th - Moon Curser - La Stella
Breakfast: Fuel up for the day with a dark roast and breakfast sandwich at Jojo's Cafe
www.jojoscafe.ca 8316 Main St (250)495-6652
Lunch: Enjoy the epic lake view at NK'MIP's Patio Restaurant
www.nkmipcellars.com 1400 Rancher Creek Rd (250)495-2985
Dinner: Tapas featuring Okanagan producers at the Restaurant at Watermark Resort
www.watermarkbeachresort.com 15 Park Pl (250)495-5508

Oliver/Golden Mile: explore Canada's wine capital
Wineries: C.C. Jentsch - Culmina - Fairview Cellars - Gehringer Brothers -Intersection - Tinhorn Creek
Lunch: Relax dolce vita style on Terrafina's patio at Hester Creek
www.terrafinarestaurant.com 887 Rd 8 (250)498-2229

Snacks: Flavourful tacos and pupusas at the bright blue roadside tables of El Sabor de Marina (next to T-2 Market)
5636 Highway 97
BBQ anyone? Follow the smoke to Hammer's House of Hog shack in Lion's Park
6607 Main St (250)535-3700
Dinner: Sunset seating at the beautiful Miradoro at Tinhorn Creek Winery
www.tinhorn.com 537 Tinhorn Creek Rd (250)498-3742

Oliver/Black Sage Bench: drink to some of the best vineyard sites in the Okanagan
Wineries: Bartier Brothers - Burrowing Owl - Stoneboat - Silver Sage - River Stone
Lunch: Posh pizzas and salads at Black Hills' Vineyard Kitchen
www.blackhillswinery.com 4190 Black Sage Rd (250)498-0666
Snack: The baked-on-site artisan bread has a cult following at Platinum Bench Winery (as does the Gamay Noir)
www.platinumbench.com 4120 Black Sage Rd (250)535-1165
Dinner: Has to be the Sonora Room at Burrowing Owl, with a knock-out view over the whole valley
www.bovwine.ca 500 Burrowing Owl Pl 1(877)498-0620

Okanagan Falls/Skaha Bench: breathe in the fresh country air, and watch the sun set through Ponderosa pine trees
Wineries: Blue Mountain - Liquidity - Meyer Family Vineyards - Synchromesh (check to confirm it's not sold out) - Wild Goose - Painted Rock
Lunch: Casual wine country BBQ on Wild Goose's Smoke and Oak Bistro patio
wildgoosewinery.com 2145 Sun Valley Way, OK Falls
(250) 497-8919
Snack: Visit old school local's fave Tickleberry's for ice cream
www.tickleberrys.com 1207 Main St, OK Falls (250)497-8862
Dinner: Admire the art while watching the sunset over Vaseux Lake at lovely Liquidity Bistro
www.liquiditywines.com 4720 Allendale Rd, OK Falls
(778)515-5500 ext1

Penticton/Naramata: the perfect spot to visit conveniently close wineries and take in the ever-present lake view
Wineries: Deep Roots - JoieFarm - Van Westen - Lake Breeze - La Frenz - Poplar Grove

Breakfast: Stop in to The Bench Market for an expertly made latte and a breakfast burrito, plus deli picnic supplies
www.thebenchmarket.com 368 Vancouver Ave, Penticton (250)492-2222

Lunch: Perfectly rustic wood-fired pizzas at JoieFarm's Picnique
www.joiefarm.com 2825 Naramata Rd, Naramata (250)496-0092

Snack: Enjoy a scrumptious cheese platter with a glass of Chard at Upper Bench Winery & Creamery
www.upperbench.ca 170 Upper Bench Rd S, Penticton (250)770-1733

Dinner: Relax with an upscale dinner on the second story deck of Hillside Winery's Bistro
www.hillsidewinery.ca 1350 Naramata Rd, Naramata (250)493-6274

Summerland/Peachland: an organic haven filled with small craft producers

Wineries: Sumac Ridge - Silkscarf Winery - Summergate Winery - Okanagan Crush Pad - Sage Hills Estate - Hainle Vineyards & Deep Creek

Breakfast: Cute bakery and coffee stop at True Grain Bread
www.truegrain.ca 10108 Main St, Summerland (250)494-4244
Tasty treats on the Peachland boardwalk at Bliss Bakery
www.blissbakery.ca 4200 Beach Ave, Peachland (250)767-2711

Lunch: Stunning views and tasty food at Evolve's restaurant
www.evolvecellars.com 20623 McDougald Rd, Summerland (778)516-7728

Dinner: Stellar lakeside location with great wine list at Local Lounge • Grille
www.thelocalgroup.ca 12817 Lakeshore Dr S, Summerland (250)494-8855

West Kelowna: big names and hidden gems

Wineries: The Hatch Wines - Rollingdale Winery - Off the Grid Organic Winery - Indigenous World Winery - Mission Hill - Quail's Gate

Breakfast: Pick up a bannock breakfast sandwich or sweet glazed bannock, and coffee at Kekuli Café
www.kekulicafe.com 3041 Louie Dr (250)768-3555

Lunch: An elegant ambiance next to the vineyards at Old Vines Restaurant in Quail's Gate Winery
www.quailsgate.com 3303 Boucherie Rd (250)769-4451

Dinner: A stunning setting and memorable experience at Mission Hill's Terrace Restaurant
www.missionhillwinery.com 1730 Mission Hill Rd (250)768-6467

East Kelowna: marquis producers, impressive tasting bars
Wineries: CedarCreek - Sandhill Wines - Spierhead Winery - Kitsch Wines -Summerhill - Tantalus
Breakfast: Sandrine French Pastry & Chocolate is a charming patisserie with excellent croissants (in Orchard Place)
www.sandrinepastry.com 1865 Dilworth Dr (250)860-1202
Lunch: Farm to table dining at the best winery restaurant in the area, CedarCreek's open air Vineyard Terrace
www.cedarcreek.bc.ca 5445 Lakeshore Rd (778)738-1027
Dinner: High calibre seasonal Okanagan cuisine at Waterfront Wines
www.waterfrontrestaurant.ca 1180 Sunset Dr (250)979-1222

Lake Country: a scenic stop where the water's never far from view
Wineries: 50th Parallel - Arrowleaf Cellars - Gray Monk Estate Winery
Breakfast: Pop into artsy and casual Lake Country Coffee House for a quick bite before exploring the wineries
10356 Bottom Wood Lake Rd, Winfield (250)766-9006
Lunch: Tuck into some antipasti, charcuterie or pizza at Ex Nihilo Vineyards' Chaos Bistro
www.exnihilovineyards.com 1525 Camp Rd, Lake Country (250)766-5522
Dinner: Gray Monk's Grapevine has a well deserved reputation as the nicest restaurant in Lake Country, with gorgeous views
www.grapevinerestaurant.ca 1055 Camp Rd, Okanagan Centre (250)766-3168

MAPS

Tip: use the trip planner at www.winebc.com/plan to organize your route.

Okanagan Valley

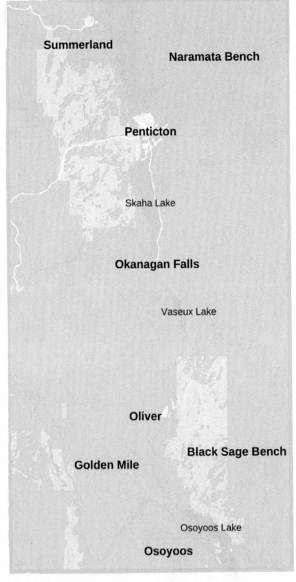

Summerland

Naramata Bench

Penticton

Skaha Lake

Okanagan Falls

Vaseux Lake

Oliver

Black Sage Bench

Golden Mile

Osoyoos Lake

Osoyoos

Southern Okanagan Valley

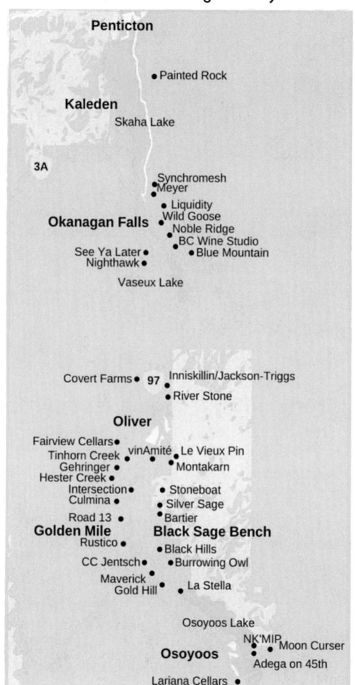

Penticton

● Painted Rock

Kaleden

Skaha Lake

3A

Synchromesh
●Meyer
● Liquidity
Wild Goose
Okanagan Falls ●
●Noble Ridge
●BC Wine Studio
See Ya Later ● ●●Blue Mountain
Nighthawk ●

Vaseux Lake

Covert Farms● **97** Inniskillin/Jackson-Triggs
●
●River Stone

Oliver

Fairview Cellars●
Tinhorn Creek ● vinAmité ● Le Vieux Pin
Gehringer ● ●●Montakarn
Hester Creek ●
Intersection● ● Stoneboat
Culmina ● ● Silver Sage
Road 13 ● ●Bartier
Golden Mile **Black Sage Bench**
Rustico ● ●Black Hills
CC Jentsch● ●Burrowing Owl
Maverick ●
Gold Hill ● ● La Stella

Osoyoos Lake

NK'MIP
●● Moon Curser
Osoyoos ●
Adega on 45th

Lariana Cellars ●

Northern Okanagan Valley

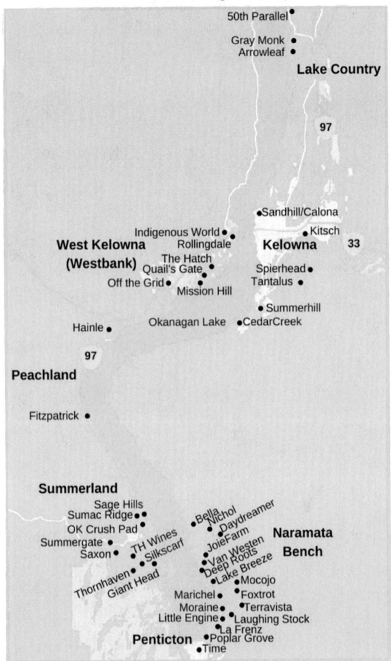

50th Parallel •

Gray Monk •
Arrowleaf •

Lake Country

97

•Sandhill/Calona
• Kitsch

Indigenous World • •
Rollingdale   **Kelowna**   33
West Kelowna
(Westbank)   The Hatch
Quail's Gate •   Spierhead •
Off the Grid •   Tantalus •
Mission Hill

• Summerhill

Hainle •   Okanagan Lake   •CedarCreek

97

Peachland

Fitzpatrick •

Summerland
Sage Hills
Sumac Ridge • •
OK Crush Pad •   Bella
Nichol
Summergate •   Daydreamer
TH Wines
Saxon •   JoieFarm   **Naramata**
Silkscarf   Van Westen   **Bench**
Thornhaven   Deep Roots
Giant Head   •Lake Breeze
•Mocojo
Marichel •   •Foxtrot
Moraine •   •Terravista
Little Engine • •Laughing Stock
La Frenz
Penticton •Poplar Grove
•Time

Similkameen Valley

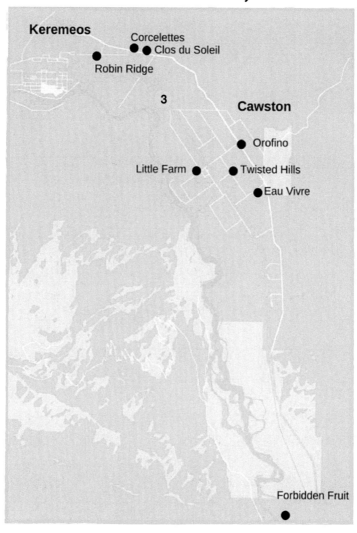

Keremeos

Corcelettes
Clos du Soleil
Robin Ridge

3

Cawston

Orofino

Little Farm
Twisted Hills
Eau Vivre

Forbidden Fruit

NOTES

DAY 1 ITINERARY

_____
_____
_____
_____
_____

DAY 2 ITINERARY

_____
_____
_____
_____
_____

DAY 3 ITINERARY

_____
_____
_____
_____
_____

MY FAVOURITE WINES

1.

2.

3.

BEST RED WINE

_____

BEST WHITE WINE

_____

BEST SPARKLING WINE

_____

BEST FORTIFIED WINE

_____

MY FAVOURITE WINERIES

1.

2.

3.

BEST VIEW

_____

BEST TASTING ROOM

_____

BEST WINERY TOUR

_____

BEST WINERY RESTAURANT

_____

GRAPES I'VE TRIED

__ ARNEIS

__ BACCHUS

__ CABERNET FRANC

__ CABERNET SAUVIGNON

__ CARMENERE

__ CHARDONNAY

__ CHENIN BLANC

__ EHRENFELSER

__ GAMAY NOIR

__ GEWURZTRAMINER

__ GRENACHE

__ GRUNER VELTLINER

__ KERNER

__ MALBEC

__ MARECHAL FOCH

__ MARSANNE

__ MARSELAN

__ MERLOT

__ MUSCAT FAMILY

__ ORTEGA

__ PETIT VERDOT

__ PINOT BLANC

__ PINOT GRIS/PINOT GRIGIO

__ PINOT NOIR

__ PINOTAGE

__ RIESLING

__ ROUSSANNE

__ SANGIOVESE

__ SAUVIGNON BLANC

__ SCHONBURGER

__ SEMILLON

__ SYRAH/SHIRAZ

__ TEMPRANILLO

__ TREBBIANO

__ VIDAL BLANC

__ VIOGNIER

__ ZINFANDEL

__ ZWEIGELT

INDEX OF WINERIES

42389032R00084

Made in the USA
San Bernardino, CA
03 December 2016